THE

GLOBAL

ENGINEER

HOW TO USE THE ESSENCE OF ENGINEERING TO BE AN ENGINEER OF INTERNATIONAL ABILITY

THE

GLOBAL

ENGINEER

HOW TO USE THE ESSENCE OF ENGINEERING TO BE AN ENGINEER OF INTERNATIONAL ABILITY

By

Clint Steele B.Eng MEI PhD

evolve Global Publishing
www.evolveglobalpublishing.com.au

The Global Engineer

1st Edition. 2023 - v3
ASIN: B0CQC5MGQT (Amazon Kindle)
ISBN: 978-0-6486232-1-2 (Amazon Paperback)
ISBN: 978-0-6486232-3-6 (Amazon Hardcover)
ISBN: 978-0-6486232-0-5 (Ingram Spark) PAPERBACK
ISBN: 978-0-6486232-2-9 Ingram Spark) HARDCOVER
ISBN: 978-0-6486231-9-9 (Smashwords)

CONTACT THE AUTHOR:
Author Website: www.cjsteele.com
Main Website: www.cjsteele.com/globalengineer.html
LinkedIn: https://www.linkedin.com/in/clint-steele

evolve Global Publishing
www.evolveglobalpublishing.com.au

Table of Contents

Foreword

This is a unique book. I wrote it because I have come to realise that there is little effort put into teaching engineering students (or practising engineers for that matter) techniques that help them think like an engineer.

I have read a number of books about engineering – especially on its history. Some of these do at least put forward interesting theories about what engineering is. However, none take the time to use these theories to actually help the reader become a better engineer. And on the topic of the essence of engineering and how to use this to be a global engineer, the literature is silent.

It seems most people simply hope that by studying engineering, doing a few practical assignments and working for a few years, they will pick things up. For many of us, this works – to an extent. However, it does raise some questions:

- How do you know you have acquired the right experience?
- What if your job doesn't allow you to develop all the skills?
- How would you know if you've missed some key skills?
- How would you know if another engineer had the same skill set as you if they'd worked elsewhere (or even with you)?
- Can you tell if experience in one area has provided you with skills suitable for another area?
- How do you know if you would be just as good an engineer elsewhere in the world?

The current state of most people's understanding of engineering thinking and engineering practice makes it difficult for one to even know what engineering is. And if you don't really know what engineering is, then how can you be certain how good an engineer you are; or know how to be the best engineer that you can be?

In this book, I am going to do two things. First, I am going to summarise what engineering is. This will be my opinion to an extent, but it will be based on the history of engineering, the actual word 'engineering', what is known about how engineers think, and research that I have conducted into engineering practice. I am then going to talk about how you can take specific action to improve your engineering ability. With this knowledge, you will be able to tell how good an engineer you are and develop the essence of engineering within yourself. Then, no matter where you are working, you will know that you are the engineer for the job at hand – you will be a global engineer.

After reading this book, you will have no doubt about what engineering is and know what you can do to continually improve your engineering ability.

Now, at this stage you're probably asking yourself: Why should I listen to you about this, Clint? And that's a very good question. I will tell you more about myself later. However, for now, I can say that I have spent the past few years researching specifically how background affects engineering skill and what can be done to improve that ability – this has come from my natural interests and my job as a researcher.

This book is essentially a redaction of what I and others have found when studying engineering and how people become good at what they do. Much of this information is not easy for the typical engineer to find. I am essentially a complier of knowledge that is already had – even though some of the knowledge was found by me. However, I am presenting this information in a manner that makes it easy for you to use.

Given my interest and knowledge in the area, compiling the information that I have found on engineering and how to be a global engineer into an easy to use format, like a book, was an obvious thing for me to do.

I have done my best to ensure that the book will help you become a global engineer. However, while I have attempted to write it in a manner that is accessible to all, I have likely written it with a bias toward helping people who think like me. You might find some parts of the book require re-reads – especially if you and I think about things in a different way from each other.

Also note the website mentioned at the end of the book. This will provide other avenues (maybe more suited to you) to help you become a global engineer.

Do you have thoughts that you would like to share about this book?

I always appreciate people taking the time to give feedback on my work. If you would like to share your thoughts on what you read here, then please take the time to contact me. This will help improve future versions.

About the Author

Why listen to Clint Steele?

I have done my best to ensure that everything in this book is well-reasoned and well-supported so that you know it is something that will help you improve your engineering ability. However, it helps to know more about the person that you are taking advice from, so I thought it would be a good idea to go over this first. This will be a bit of a biography, so if you're not too big a fan of hearing people's life stories, and you just want to get to the useful stuff, then, by all means, skip this section.

I was not born wanting to be an engineer.

When I was younger, I actually had little idea what I wanted to do career wise and, as a result, I went through a few ideas: fitter and turner because that is what my father was; chef because I loved eating and learned to cook at a young age; TV reviewer because I also loved watching TV; police officer because the cops on TV seemed to have an exciting life; electrician because they were paid well and the work was not too hard; maybe even crane operator because it too paid well and my cousin did it. Only recently I found out that it's possible to be a professional Lego builder – if I'd known that some decades ago....

This lack of direction had a serious effect on how well I went at school. Throughout the early years, I was almost always in some special class for kids who weren't getting it. I usually did well in mathematics and I always did well when it was time to write stories, but my English skills left a bit to be desired. Every report card said that I was easily distracted. Unless I enjoyed it or could see some benefit (and I rarely could), then I never really wanted to do any schoolwork. Once I was in secondary education, I was always worried that I might be kept back a year and studied hard enough to just pass. Mathematics was still saving me and anything related to writing was a complete failure, except for mythology because I liked the topic.

Dramatic change came at the age of 14 when, on a family holiday, bored out of my head in the bush with my family, I came across a hot-rod magazine. If I recall correctly, it was bought to help alleviate boredom for me or my brother. This particular magazine was fairly heavy on technical issues. It still had pictorials of all these customised cars, but it also had sections on how to get more out of a car's engine and suspension system. It was not the notion of going fast that got my attention so much as the idea that you could be strategic in the way you put a car together if you knew how everything worked. It was that idea of using the knowledge of mechanisms (that I later learned was basically physics) to actually determine how a car would perform that captivated me. That was when I decided I was going to be one of those people who designed cars.

So who were these people? Engineers, I was told. How do you become an engineer? You need to study at university. What do I need to do to get into an engineering course at university? You will need to study mathematics and science subjects in high school and do reasonably well at them.

It is amazing what a difference a little motivation can have. I never did that well in any other subject related to literature or art in high school, but I did well enough to get into an engineering degree. After this experience, I realised how hard school can be for a young person who doesn't know what they want to do afterwards. If you do have direction and know where you're going, then count yourself very lucky. Not many of us have that.

I was lucky enough to go to a university that required a total of 12 months industry-based engineering experience before graduation. I was lucky again to get work positions in design and development, which was all that engineering was – as far as I was concerned at that time. Not only that, but I got my chance to experience the auto industry to see how it operated. I also worked for a smaller company that made soft rock drilling equipment. Because of the size of the second company and the high turnaround rate required, I was able to see a number of my designs made and used by the customer. I got to see a few of them come back for changes too. It was only 12 months, but it certainly did a lot to develop my engineering design skills. It also made me think about what actually made for a good engineer. If you ever have a chance to work as an engineer while still studying, then take it. The work experience will make it much easier to understand the importance of your course content, and this will motivate you in your studies.

It was in the final year of my undergraduate studies that I was introduced to probabilistic design. The lecturer was ex-Xerox, which had been heavily involved in the transfer of quality ideas from Japan to the US and also conducted some of its own research into design for quality. The essence or goal of probabilistic design was robustification – where a design is optimised so that it is less sensitive to errors from manufacturing, wear or random effects from the environment. Given that this was an extension to the whole concept of using one's understanding of a system to tune it so that it performed better, I was hooked, and I enrolled in a PhD, which I started the following year. That took a long time.

After all that study, it was time to enter 'the real world'. Once again, I was pretty lucky to get another role in design and development. It actually took a while; I got quite a lot of knockbacks from companies that were sure I was not going practical enough given that I had a PhD.

All those rejections were actually good for me. The job I ended up with not only involved a lot of design and development, but it also involved production issues, quality and warranty issues, and service issues. The best thing about that aspect of the job was that it showed me the diversity of jobs that engineers could do while also showing what was common to all . There was another aspect to the job that was informative: the people I worked with. Even though it was a small company, it took its engineering seriously, and there was a diversity of engineers that I was fortunate to call colleagues. I recall an engineer who was successful because of his tenacity – no matter the issue, he just wouldn't give up until he found the solution and he was sure it was the right one. Another engineer was incredibly thorough, and all decisions were well founded and almost impossible to question. There was also an engineer who had worked in the same role for years and developed a collection of near unconscious guides in his mind that could help inform all his design decisions. And then there was an engineer who would come up with a basic idea, make it and then tune it until it worked. This is just a sample of the engineers that I worked with – so you get an idea of diversity within engineering this role exhibited to me.

This diversity was nothing compared to what I was going to see next.

For a year or so a university friend had been asking me to work for his company in China. He had a design consultancy. He was getting the customers, but he had issues with the Chinese engineers understanding what the western clients wanted. I had been to India and South East Asia, but never China, so I was keen. However, each time he asked, I was in the middle of something that needed completing in my current role. Soon enough though, there was an opportunity, and I took it.

Sometimes we like to think that engineering is universal, but I can tell you from personal experience, and as I argue in this book, that it is not. The basic end goal is the same, but the way it is viewed and the way it is achieved can vary. And this variation can cause some serious issues.

I could not put my finger on what it was, but when I was in China, there was something different about the work. You just couldn't be sure that you were on the same page as the other engineers. The only thing that got me through was that I had had enough experience to realise that you need to find numerous ways to double check that everyone thinks the same thing. It was like feedforward versus feedback control. When you're in your own culture, you can use feedforward. You can just say whatever is on your mind and be pretty sure the message is understood. But when you're in another culture, you need to always make sure you get feedback to ensure that the understanding is correct. If it isn't, then you send a slightly different message and check that. I also noticed that some people just couldn't do this without first having an aneurysm. I knew how to survive in a different culture as an engineer, but I really didn't know why there was a difference in engineering in the first place.

I planned on staying in China for two years or more, but the global financial crisis put a stop to that. The customer base dried up, and there was no work for me. So back home it was.

This was another period of unemployment. However, serendipity raised her head again. At the same time, the role for the engineering design lecturer (or professor, depending upon the university you are at) at a university became available and it was recommended to me by one of the other lecturers there. Given that I had a PhD, experience teaching and experience in design, I got the job. However, it meant that I needed to find some research topics.

I could recall going to a lecture some years prior where the presenter was talking about the change in focus on engineering research. The change was toward the way engineers think, and developing these skills earlier in engineering students instead of just hoping such skills will develop some years after graduation. I was also wondering about why there was a difference in engineering between countries. And why some engineers could work with others while some could not.

And there was my research topic – what makes engineers think a certain way and how do we develop engineering wisdom?

Having a topic to research was one thing, but now I needed to work out what had been done and how I was going to add to that research. I had always had an interest in engineering practice, theory and research, but understanding what had been done and working out how I was going to become active in this area needed more than just an interest.

The first thing that really brought me to writing this book was a paper by the researcher Nigel Cross. It was about engineering design expertise. In this paper, the author summarised interviews with two world-class engineers and identified the three characteristics that they had in common and that made them expert engineers. Based on my own experience, I could see how these characteristics were common to the good engineers that I had worked with, but not developed to a level that they could be. Probably because the engineers didn't know that they could or should develop these three characteristics within themselves. At that point, I knew the kinds of things I needed to develop in my students. The question then was: how?

The second thing that made me decide to share what I know about engineering was my research into Chinese and western design teams. It actually dawned on me after I was reading the interview summary with a Canadian electrical engineer who, at the time, worked in China, and thinking about what a Chinese friend had said to me about his thoughts on why there was a difference. It suddenly became apparent how the western background made western engineers think and operate in a way that was different from the way a Chinese background made Chinese engineers think and operate. It was good to come to that realisation, but the more fundamental implication was that a good portion of our engineering skill is a result of our background. That means we do not need to simply accept our ability as it is. Instead, we can work to make ourselves better engineers.

Now that I knew how backgrounds affected engineering ability, I was able to try ways of developing key skills in my students. This led to more research into teaching engineering wisdom to engineering students. I discovered these keys to being a better and global engineer somewhat by accident. That's probably why not many others (no-one as far as I can tell – it seems I am the only one who has researched how background affects engineering behaviour) share this knowledge with other engineers. Those who do know about this have only stumbled across it by luck. However, once you get it, it is easy to improve your ability. I figured there is nothing but benefits from sharing this. And that is why this book was written.

1.

Introduction

Let's talk about engineering.

1.1 What is engineering?

Chances are that if you're reading this book, then you're either an engineer or studying to become one. This means you know what engineering is. Nevertheless, you might still have some uncertainty about the exact nature of engineering.

Even though engineers themselves know what engineering is when they see it, they are typically unable to explain what engineering is to others.

If you can't explain engineering to others, then do you really know what it is? I think you do, but it would be good for us to have a shared definition for this book. There are many definitions out there about what engineering is. Personally, I think they are overly complicated and excessively long. They are frequently trying to explain the diversity of what engineers do, but they don't focus on what is common to all these activities. They don't capture the essence of engineering.

A note on the diverse practices of engineering

In practice, engineers do much more than engineering. They need to communicate, they need to manage, they need to perform administrative tasks and they must also perform many other duties that are not explicitly engineering. Similar things can be said of other professions too. Accountants do not count all day, chefs need to keep track of kitchen expenses and teachers need to complete quality-control paperwork. Every role will have many activities that are not unique to the related profession. This book is not about the professional skills that all engineers (and other professionals) need. There are plenty of books on that topic. This book is about those skills that are unique to engineering.

After thinking about this for some years, I have found that the best way to explain engineering is through etymology. You might be wondering what etymology is. Not to worry – we engineers are rarely noted for our broad vocabularies. Etymology is the study of the history of words. No surprise if you, an engineer, didn't know that. I had to look it up too when I started investigating what engineering is and how to be a better engineer.

The history of the word 'engineering' (its etymology) is both informative and something that every engineer should know. Just think about it – being an engineer and not even knowing where the word for your profession comes from. That's not good.

The word 'engineering' comes from the Latin *ingenium*, which essentially means ingenuity from which comes 'ingenious'. 'Ingenious' is one of my favourite words. It basically means being creative and practical at the same time. There's nothing ingenious about a creative idea that can't work, nor is there anything ingenious about simply doing what you know works because you've done it many times in the past.

Note: while there's nothing ingenious about reinventing the wheel, there's also nothing ingenious about ignoring an existing solution to a problem if you know it's the best solution. This is a paradox in engineering that all engineers need to wrestle with.

Being ingenious, I think, and I hope you agree, is the essential characteristic of what engineers do. Because we have this essence of engineering, we now have something that we can use as a foundation of what engineering is. And we can use that as a foundation for becoming better engineers.

engineering [en-j uh - neer -ing]

(verb) the formulation of an ingenious solution to a given problem

This definition is short and manages to encompass all that engineers do.

To be ingenious, one needs to be creative, which is something engineers should be. Also, there would be nothing ingenious about ignoring theory that can help one better understand a problem or refine a solution. This is why, as engineers, we study scientific theory. It would also be ingenious to be aware of external factors that affect the success of a proposed solution, and this is why engineers also study management, ethics and business theory. Everything that an engineer learns allows them the ability to be ingenious, which is what makes them engineers.

Note the use of the word 'everything'. Some engineers seem to forget much of what they are taught. I will explain later why this is an issue.

I am pretty sure that you will be happy with the definition above. However, not many people would come up with such a definition. This is because of how the rest of the world sees engineering. The majority of languages within continental Europe have a word for 'engineer' that starts with an 'I', and communicates the origin of the word. Thus, it is perhaps no surprise that it is Europe that is often associated with excellence in engineering – Europeans seem to have a better appreciation of what engineering actually is.

The meaning of 'engineer' in many other parts of the world is not what we, as engineers, might prefer.

In the English language, the word 'engineer' can mean *one who operates an engine and understands how it works*. Many years ago, my mother worked for a company that conducted market research. She was instructed to always double-check the details of someone's job when they said they were an engineer. They were often train-engine drivers, mechanics or machine tool operators, such as machinists or turners.

In Chinese, the characters that are used to make up the word engineer — 工程师 — mean 'labour', 'regulation' and 'teacher' respectively. We need to be careful with how we interpret Chinese characters because bringing two or more characters together can remove the meanings of the individual characters. I worked as an engineer in China for a year before I fully appreciated this nuance of Chinese. However, I also noticed that while engineers were highly regarded in China, the Chinese word itself did encourage a regulatory attitude towards what engineering was to be and how it was viewed.

Through a conversation I had with a fellow engineer on LinkedIn, I found that the Hindi word for 'engineer' is *abhiyanta*, which is derived from two Sanskrit words, *a-bhay* and *yantra*. These words mean 'fearless' and 'contraption'/'gadget' respectively. Basically, the Hindi word for engineer means *one who is comfortable with gadgets*.

These three words (the English, the Chinese and the Hindi) show aspects of professional engineering that are true but ignore the essence of engineering — ingenuity.

The limiting words sometimes used as nouns for those who practise engineering have resulted in a poor attitude toward engineering and a lack of appreciation for what engineering truly is. This lack of understanding has permeated many aspects of engineering: education, management, society's perception and even the self-identity of engineers (do you automatically think of yourself as ingenious?). This poor attitude has in turn contributed to engineers not actively developing those key skills that help them to be ingenious. This poses a key question; one this book will answer:

What can an engineer do to increase their ingenuity, and think even more like an excellent and global engineer so they too become such an engineer?

1.2 What is engineering design?

As with engineering, you probably have a sense of what engineering design is, but can't really explain it. Once again, I think using etymology helps. The word 'design' comes from the Latin *designare*, meaning to mark out or designate. It was the word 'designate' that 'design' was originally associated with when it was introduced into the English language.

> **engineering design**
>
> (verb) the designation of the final form of an ingenious idea so that it can be implemented.

The above definition does not state how the designation process is to take place. It could be done through sketching, mathematical modelling, via the outcome of trials and testing, or any of the other methods used by engineers and designers. However, this definition does show that an idea alone is not enough. The idea needs to be fully defined and designated so it can be implemented.

While I am content with the definition above, I do think we need to remember that design is integral to engineering. If there is no actual design, then what does engineering become? It would be nothing more than the collection of knowledge and ideas, and no actual implementation – that's not engineering. Thus, we can say that all engineers are also designers. We might design project plans, manufacturing jigs, operating instructions, and more. These things might not be what you think of when you think of engineering design, but they are all designs nonetheless. Because, before we design them, or designate their form, they are just ideas that cannot yet be implemented.

Design skills are essential to being an engineer.

'Design' in other languages

This is something I learned when I was in China and have found to be fairly common around the world. Many bilingual dictionaries were written after 'design' acquired its more varied meaning, which includes a reference to aesthetics and style. Because of this, the accepted translations into other languages will often refer to art, beauty, fashion, and other aesthetic efforts. This can cause confusion when talking with others about engineering design. You might sometimes need to take time to explain what is meant by 'design' when talking about engineering design in other parts of the world. I know I have had to do this a few times – Turkish and Armenian come to mind first. Explaining the origin and how the meaning changed before bilingual dictionaries were written helps with this explanation. It seems there are really no other languages that have a true equivalent of the word 'design' in its most varied use.

1.3 How can understanding design make you a better engineer?

There is actually a lot of research out there on how people design (including engineering design). Not many realise this – assuming design is just done. This research focuses on how people design and how they can be better designers, which carries over to being a better engineer.

Unfortunately, this research does not often make it into engineering education. Also, many books on engineering design focus on machine design or the management of the design process. These areas are important, but they do little to actually help you be a better engineer. What's worse, many of these books are written in a manner that makes them hard to use. They are written to impress academics; not to educate the reader. Thus, even if there is something within these texts that could help you, then it has probably been written in such a convoluted manner that you are likely to miss it.

However, by understanding what we already know about engineering design in practice and how it works, you will be enabled to review your own skills. You can then use this knowledge to effectively guide your efforts to improve those skills. This is where engineering design is clearly different from other engineering topics. You can master theory associated with topics such as materials, statics, and heat transfer. There is only so much knowledge that we possess or really need to possess about the scientific engineering topics. However, design is a skill (not just knowledge and theory to be understood) and as yet we do not know how far this skill can be developed.

In fact, there is no known limit to how good an engineer you can be through improved engineering design skills.

What is known is that skills, such as engineering skill, can be improved through dedicated practice. Our understanding of engineering design provides insights into how you can practice while working to continually become a better engineer (even if you do not consider yourself to be a design engineer). And that's what I want to share with you.

1.4 What this book will do for you

In this book, I am going to explain what we know about engineering design. Unlike other texts on engineering, I am going to do my best to make things as clear, as useful and practical as possible.

As I mentioned above, many engineering texts are made to sound more complex than they need to be. This is simply so the author can show off to other academics (or to make other academics think that the book must be good because it sounds more complicated than something that they would write). I am quite confident that what I have here is unique and extremely useful in making you a better engineer, regardless of your experience. So I feel no need to show off with convoluted sentences – apologies in advance if it ever seems that way.

After reading this book, you will be able to understand your strengths and weaknesses as an engineer. With this understanding we can then look at how you can change the way you think and approach problems so that you are a better engineer. At the end, you will understand yourself (and others) as an engineer. And you will then be on the path of continually improving yourself as an engineer.

In fact, it is quite likely that before you even get to the end of the book you will have:

- Already developed some key skills in engineering cognition.
- Noticed that you can make yourself think in a different manner (more like a global engineer).

- Become a better engineer and know why.

- Become able to apply your engineering skill in any context around the globe.

- Started spotting nuances in others engineers and noticed how they could improve.

At the very least, after you have read this, you will know that you do indeed have a good understanding of what makes a good engineer and that you are one who is now better able to work globally.

2.

Being an Excellent Engineer

There is plenty known about being an excellent engineer. What is known, as you will see, is independent of culture, nationality or organizational context. It is therefore inherently global. By first understanding the essence of excellent engineering, you will have the perfect foundation for being a global engineer.

Excellence in engineering is the best place to start when becoming a global engineer.

In this chapter, I am going to go over the basics of what is known about engineering cognition. This will show you what you want to aim for. If you don't know what you need to become an excellent engineer, then no matter how hard you try, you will be unlikely to drive your efforts in the correct direction. At the end of this chapter, you will know what attributes you need to work on to become the best engineer you possibly can be. You will then be in the best position to become a global engineer.

2.1 The essentials

One of the most obvious ways to work out what makes an excellent engineer is to look at those who have achieved the most and see what they have in common. Any commonality would be the essence of engineering expertise. Once this is known, you or I (or any other engineer - say someone you mentor for example) can then go about developing this same essence within.

This exact research into engineering excellence was actually done and reported upon in the now classic paper written by Nigel Cross and Anita Clayburn Cross (1998). This paper documents research into two expert engineers. One was Gordon Murray – an English Formula 1 engineer involved in many of the innovations of Formula 1 in the 1970s and 1980s. The other was Victor Scheinman – an American engineer who has received numerous awards for his engineering over a number of years. What was unique about this work was that it was focused on engineers who were clearly the best in their fields. Most other research into engineering skill and expertise relied upon the typical engineer or a comparison between an experienced engineer and a student engineer. It would be hoped that the experienced engineer was suitably capable, but this is never really known. Therefore, studying two truly exceptional engineers, like Gordon Murray and Victor Scheinman, provided insights into what it is that can make all of us better engineers. I will not say more about what these two engineers have achieved because it would take a while and you can easily read more about them elsewhere if you wish – they are famous enough to be well-documented on the internet. Also, it is the lessons that we learn from them that are most important to us at this time. Still, I recommend that you look them up; it's always good to learn about how other engineers work (a habit you should develop).

This research into these two expert engineers found that the following three practices were common:

- framing
- systemic thinking
- the application of first principles.

Not only were these practices common to the two expert engineers, they had also been noticed in others. The fact that they were so pronounced in these two shows that they are the most important practices. If you can master these practices, then you are well on your way to being an exceptional engineer.

But what are they exactly? That's what I am going to talk about now.

2.1.1 Framing

I personally find framing incredibly interesting. It is the one of the three attributes that is hardest to fully understand, but we all do it and can tell when we have. That means that once you get your head around what framing is, you will easily be able to tell when you are doing it and also notice when you are getting better at it.

Framing is basically working out what the real problem is. In your case, framing means working out what the engineering problem is. People will come to you with their problem, but you need to work out what the engineering problem is — the problem that you will solve. This is called framing because it is like choosing the window (or frame) through which you will look at the problem. I am going to talk about this a lot more later, but for now, it is important that you appreciate two basic things about framing:

1. It can involve removing the original frame first.
2. There can often be more than one frame, and you need to choose the one you will use.

One of the best illustrations of framing I have noted comes from Gordon Murray.

During Gordon's time as an F1 engineer, a requirement of ground clearance was introduced. This requirement stipulated that the clearance under a car would need to be 6 cm. Such a gap under an F1 car would practically eliminate the ground effect that was used to provide extra downforce during cornering. When cornering, a downforce larger than the mass of the car allows for much greater speed. This problem actually caused Gordon Murray some worry for some time. How could a ground effect be achieved with such a large gap? This would seem to be an insoluble aerodynamics problem.

The solution that came to Gordon was to actually view the problem as a suspension problem, and not an aerodynamics one.

The use of active suspension had already been banned, so the use of something controlled by the driver was not an option. Therefore, Gordon hit upon the idea of designing a suspension system that would be pulled down by the downward aerodynamic force, that was generated at higher speeds, to a height that would allow for the desired ground effect. If the speed reduced, then the suspension system would return to the original height. However, the speed of return would be slow enough so that the ground effect remained during the slower cornering. Thus, during inspection, the car would have the required 6 cm clearance, but during racing, that clearance would be lower.

This is an excellent example of framing because it shows that the original frame sometimes needs to be removed. It was originally viewed as an aerodynamics problem, but was turned into a suspension design problem. It also shows creativity, which, as I will discuss later, can help with framing. Finally, it actually provides a guide for further development work. It is possible that there were other equally valid frames that would have brought about a desirable outcome. However, by choosing this one it was possible to move forward, which is sometimes more important – something else I will talk about later.

Not only are there many possible frames, but a chosen frame might also prove to be unsuitable for a given problem, and you will need to go back and start again. As you progress in solving an engineering problem, you begin to see how the approach you have taken will not work. You then need to think about the problem differently. This often seems like a waste of time. However, you did have direction, which allowed you to try something and to better understand the problem.

If you have the time, then I suggest you read *Hitting the Brakes: Engineering Design and the Production of Knowledge* by Ann Johnson. In this book, Johnson uses the development of antiskid braking systems to understand the nature of engineering knowledge. In the book, there are many examples of framing without using the word. It seems Johnson was unaware that the concept had a name when she was writing the book. Read the passage below from the book and see how the problem was often reframed as understanding was developed.

> *Thus I can trace knowledge and community evolution through a series of how questions that united the effort to design antilock systems. The nascent community initially asked, How can we reduce skidding accidents in passenger cars? The group that defined skidding as a braking problem continually refined their central question. They first asked, How can we design a braking system to prevent skidding in panic-stop situations without requiring the driver to change his or her habits? Then they asked, How can we determine that a car is about to skid so that a system can prevent skidding? How should we design an electronic system to measure imminent skidding, then a*

hydraulic system to react to that electrical signal? And finally they asked, How can we make a mass-producible electronic control system that will integrate with the braking system and prevent the car from skidding without the driver even knowing it is there? Whether the systems completely accommodate these requirements is still unclear; the question of assessment is the subject of this book's epilogue. But I want to emphasize the changing questions the community asked and show how these changes were interwoven with the changing member- ship of the knowledge community.

Note also that while the challenge is reframed, it is still stated as a question or a problem. It's not really framing as I describe it – it includes coevolution, which I will cover later. However, it is a clear example of how the community looking into antiskid braking sys- tems had to keep on 'redefining' what the real problem was as they progressed to a final solution.

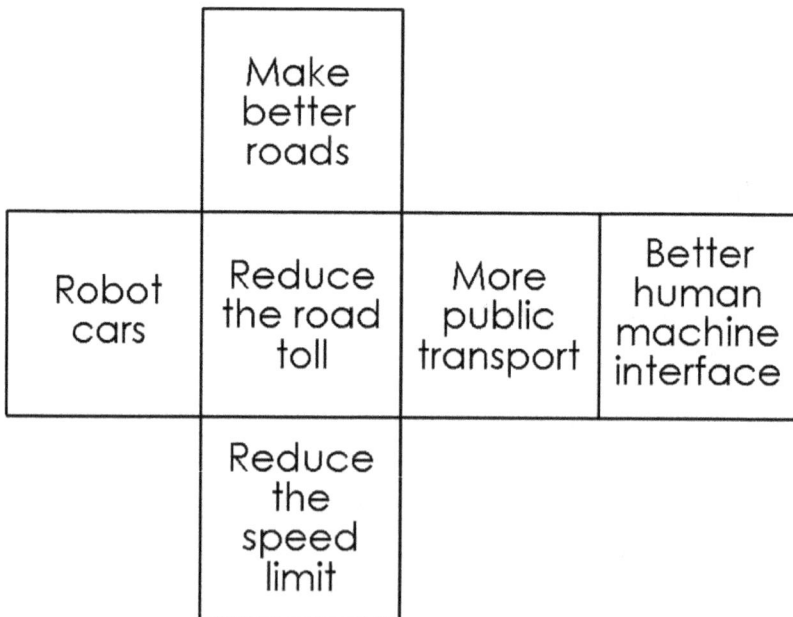

	Make better roads		
Robot cars	Reduce the road toll	More public transport	Better human machine interface
	Reduce the speed limit		

Framing is like third-angle projection: looking at the same thing but from a different perspective. The challenge to reduce the road toll might mean something like: getting people off the road with public transport; making a better control system so drivers can drive safely; reducing the kinetic energy so less damage is done; eliminating the need for a driver via a more reliable machine; or improving the roads to ensure grip. You need to decide which frame is best and work on your ability to develop that frame.

2.1.2 Systemic thinking

Firstly, systemic thinking should never be confused with systematic thinking.

Systematic thinking is where you apply the same system to your thinking each time. There are many tools for that and sometimes they can be very useful. However, systemic thinking is related more to your focus.

When you are dealing with an engineering problem, do you find that you can only deal with the precise issue at hand? Perhaps it is just one issue at a time that you can deal with. Or, are you able to think about all the different facets of the problem at one time? If you are able to consider all the different facets at one time, then you are thinking systemically. This is a better option because it allows you to properly consider all the implications of any decision you might make about a solution that you plan to implement. Otherwise, you will need to implement the solution and then see these implications.

Depending upon your professional background, education or experience, you might be familiar with terms such as concurrent engineering or simultaneous engineering. These are similar, in principle, to the essence of systemic thinking. We basically need to consider all issues at once when formulating engineering decisions. This is because a decision made about one system can affect what happens in another system and then have a very significant effect on the performance of the overall system you are working on. Remember what I said earlier about engineers sometimes forgetting what they had been taught? Now you can see why engineers need to not only learn so many things but also why they need to remember them if they wish to be good engineers. If you can't keep all the knowledge in your head, then you can't notice potential issues or opportunities outside of the system you are working on. Thus you might inadvertently cause an issue or you might miss an opportunity.

Easier said than done

Now I know, full well, that it is quite easy to say that you should think systemically. However, many people are detailed thinkers. This helps explain common engineering tools, such as the house of quality and Ishikawa fishbone diagrams – they document each detail of an engineering system and help you better understand why the system is the way it is, or why it might be failing.

I will talk more about how you can increase your ability to think systemically in chapter 3. However, for now, I will share two things with you. Firstly, your systemic thinking will become better with practise. Many people, as they get older, find that if they were detailed thinkers when younger, have become better at systemic thinking. Secondly, there are many tools that help you emulate the effects of systemic thinking. If you feel that you are weak in this attribute and you want to increase your systemic thinking ability, then take a look at mind-maps. They are especially good for those who are visual — the majority of engineers are — but help everyone. Their effectiveness at helping you perceive all the facets of any problem is remarkable and well-documented.

2.1.3 The applications of first principles

There is a reason why engineering degrees today have so many science-based subjects. In fact, you might sometimes wonder if, with all these science subjects focused on calculations and memory, you were actually ever taught to be an engineer when you were studying.

It was not always like this. Between the end of World War II and the 1960s, much of engineering education was project-based (giving design and build tasks) and aimed at helping engineers develop intuition and creativity in the face of technical problems. An engineer from such programs could turn their hand to many things and would have been very practical. However, they were not suitable for the 'space race' and the advanced technologies that were developing in the 60s and 70s.

There was an increasing need for engineering systems to be lighter, faster, stronger, cheaper and more. Because of this need, it became important for an engineer to have the scientific knowledge that allowed them to optimize a design and know that it was indeed optimal. Without a good grasp of first principles, how could this be done? In fact, when compared to all the other design professions, engineering is the only one where you need to be able to argue that your solution is the optimal one. Other designers can prove that their design looks good to a certain element of the market and then try to argue that the other elements have no taste (consider industrial design and architecture for some examples). However, if the system you produce as an engineer is less efficient, less reliable or simply less productive (and remember, these can all be measured), then there's no way you can argue that your design is acceptable. Not only that, but why would anyone choose to use your system if it could be shown to be less optimized than another? As an engineer, you need to know how to optimize your designs.

While it is the case that first principles have become more important in relatively recent times, they have always been important and an advantage to have. In the late 18th century, the French kept the method of descriptive geometry secret because of the remarkable advantage it gave their military. Descriptive geometry is an application of first principles to engineering drawings for efficient design implementation. Sometimes, the advantage is small, but because it is measurable, it is easy to see who is best and who is not. All things being equal, the engineer with the better ability to apply first principles can expect a tremendous advantage.

Unfortunately, much of the education that focuses on first principles never really teaches you how to actually apply these first principles. For some people, their entire degree is nothing but first principles (engineering science) subjects, and this can be very limiting. Confronting this lack of application can be difficult after graduation. So instead, many engineers simply start to design and implement what they have seen others do or what they found works through trial and error. They then become capable in their own areas, because they have the experience, but they can't move to other areas. They can't be true engineers. This is not to say there is no room for being a specialist. There is a lot of value in experience. I am simply pointing out that something has gone wrong when other areas of engineering endeavour seem to be a complete mystery to an engineer — you should be able to see the basics in most areas of engineering, and first principles allows for this.

An anecdote on how one graduate improved his first principles ability

I recall, some years ago now, a student calling me after he had graduated. He realised that, despite his excellent marks (the highest in his year), he had not truly learnt anything. He was unable to actually apply what he had learnt. This is a common story amongst engineering graduates from universities around the world. You have probably heard many engineers say that they have used less than 5% of what they learned when studying. You might have said it yourself. The only thing that I think is unique to this story was that this student was prepared to acknowledge that he should be able to do better, that he hadn't learned what he should, and that he should now do something about it. If all engineers were to think like this, then you would be unlikely to hear any of them say that they use less than 5% of their education.

Of all the three primary attributes, I have found this to be the most confronting for engineers. We often have to confess our ignorance — which engineers seem to rarely enjoy — if we are to improve it. Not only that, but it can also mean that a large change to the way we do our jobs if we wish to employ first principles more than we do.

Despite this challenge, it is the application of first principles that can be essential to being a true engineer. We do not need to rely on past experience alone, and be stuck in just one area for the rest of our lives. We can instead use the laws of nature themselves to understand a diversity of engineering problems that could be thrown at us, and then take these problems on with success.

We can be real engineers: ingenious.

I will, of course, talk more about improving this ability in chapter 3, but if you wish to work on it now, then the easiest thing to do is simply try the following for each engineering decision you make from now on:

1. Ask yourself what theories are important. Note the section later in this chapter about what theory is.
2. Ask what it is about the respective system that would make it optimal: what is its purpose and what is the best performance that can be expected?

3. Determine how you can use the theory to inform this decision.

It might be that you need to sit down and do some serious calculations. Or it might simply be that you can establish that bigger (or smaller) is better, and use that to inform your decision. In either case, you have improved your understanding of the situation and the quality of your decision by using first principles.

If, in Step 1, you have some issues, then you have two choices. The first is to ask a colleague what they think. Usually, it is people who have the confidence and courage to admit they do not know something who take this route. I have known engineers like this in the past, and have seen them improve very quickly and also seen them meet with much greater success. The other choice is to search through texts and websites after you have hopefully at least worked out the right keywords that will find the theory you need. The latter option is for those of us who do not like confessing our ignorance. I have worked with engineers who fall into this category too. I have noticed that they are usually brought undone by one of two things:

1. Reality.
2. A socially inept, yet helpful, colleague who innocently points out the flaw – without being asked.

Admittedly, I tend to fall into the second group unless I feel the colleague I would talk to is a recognised expert, and I figure that there is no shame in talking to them. It is something that I still need to work on. One fringe benefit I have found from asking others for advice is that it can improve your network quality considerably. Others become much more interested in your success when they feel like they have contributed to it. Having people this interested in you can help your career a lot and make it much easier to ask for a favour. It can also be an excellent way to get a mentor and if someone asks you for help it is an excellent way to become one yourself. The point I am making here is that talking about first principles and how to apply them to a situation can also be a way to build strong connections with other engineers. Given that this is on top of being a better engineer, improving your ability to apply first principles is an extremely wise pursuit.

A temptation to ignore first principles

You might be tempted at times to rely on simulations. Things like FEA (Finite Element Analysis) and CFD (Computational Fluid Dynamics) should allow for as accurate or even more accurate predictions than first principles: Surely!?! They can at times offer just this. However, they do not offer the opportunity for optimisation that a strategic application of first principles will. Thus, it can be hard to argue that your design is optimum, and that no competitor will offer a superior alternative. In addition, if you don't understand how the simulator works, then it might mislead you. You might not realise this until it is too late. Eugene S. Ferguson in *Engineering and the Mind's Eye* relays a story of an engineer who designed a structure using a simulator that did not account for buckling. In the simulator, everything looked good. However, once snow fell on the roof of the structure, and changed the loading to induce buckling, the entire structure fell like a set of dominoes. Then it was realised that the simulator had a few key assumptions within the algorithms that needed to be accounted for. There's always a reason for an engineer to use first principles.

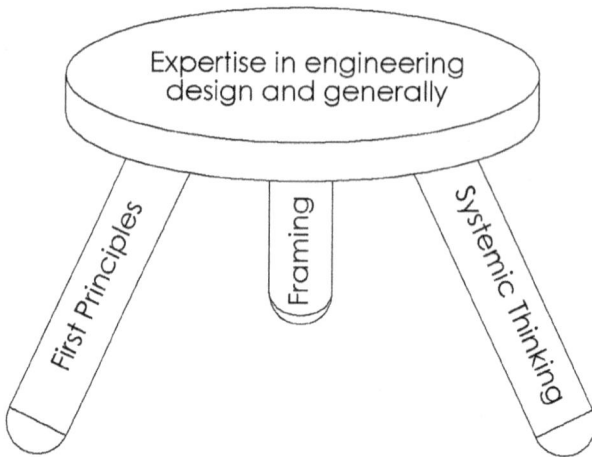

If engineering expertise were a 3 legged stool

2.2 A broader perspective on engineering excellence

There are other characteristics of the way engineers think when they take on a problem. These characteristics all stem from the fact that engineering problems, like design problems in general, are ill-defined. This makes them trickier than other problems.

The characteristics that I am going to cover here are not like the essential three attributes that I spoke about in the previous section. Instead, they are characteristics that can help you better evaluate the suitability of your design style (or even another's design style) to a particular problem so that you can improve as an engineer.

If you can:

- possess and develop the essential three attributes I have just covered,
- review the suitability of the following techniques as you approach each problem, and

- tune the application of these techniques to suit each given problem you encounter,

then you cannot help but be a better engineer.

2.2.1 Goal analysis

What should I be trying to do?

This is a question that one asks oneself when performing goal analysis. It sounds a little like framing, but there is a slight difference. Framing is more focused upon defining, or even redefining, the main problem. Goal analysis is the process of identifying or defining constraints or performance criteria. In chapter 5, I will talk about an example that shows how goal analysis tendencies can be affected by your economic and national background. However, for now, an example will help solidify your understanding of goal analysis. You will then know it when you see it and notice it when others are doing it.

> Consider two engineers who have been asked to 'optimise' the assembly of a domestic air conditioner compressor.
>
> The first engineer has looked at the workforce and noticed that there is a diversity of people with regards to size and fitness, and thus strength. Therefore, he adds a constraint to the problem definition, and adds the requirement of minimal manual force throughout the assembly to the requirements that have already been noted.
>
> The second engineer has had a lot of experience in factories where there is high transience in the workforce. In the early years of her career, she was always dealing with quality problems caused by new workers not knowing exactly what they were meant to do. For this reason, she includes a goal to mistake-proof the production process.

In each of the above cases, the engineer investigated the problem and used this to expand their understanding of the problem and to set goals to be met. This is goal analysis. It is hard to criticize either of the goals that the engineers added. However, there was evidence that the second engineer was influenced by her past experience. If her experience is similar to where she works, then this is good. However, if she is in a new industry or country, then some of her past experience might have resulted in unsuitable goal analysis – this is similar to having erroneous preconceptions.

2.2.2 Solution focusing

Sometimes, it is worth simply assuming a type of solution. This will move you quickly towards a possible solution. If you are experienced with the problem that you are working on, then the assumed solution type is probably a good one. If you've not seen such a problem before, then solution focusing might not be an option. Further, if you want a novel solution, then solution focusing might not be desirable. If this is not the case, and the speed of the solution is a major issue, then a solution focus is ideal.

A good example, I think, came from a friend's father when he was confronted by a hole in a door in his home. He was a panel-beater and automatically saw a solution that relied on the use of body putty and sheet metal. He then placed a piece of sheet metal in the hole, added the putty, sanded it back and then used his spray gun to paint the door to a nice glossy finish.

You can see from the above example that, due to his background, my friend's father focused on a type of solution. In this case it was probably not optimal. However, if we broaden our perspective on the problem to say it needed to be fixed quickly and without external help, then we could argue that this was indeed an optimum solution. Solution focusing might sound like goal analysis because the goal might be to not incur external costs. However, in the original problem, the hole simply needed to be fixed and my friend's father felt using putty, sheet metal and spray paint to fill the hole was the right solution type.

2.2.3 Coevolution

Solution focusing and goal analysis, while they can be affected by our background and might or might not be suited to the problem we are facing, are topics that lead into another topic about engineering problems called coevolution.

Coevolution is basically the natural result of the nature of the problems that engineers often face.

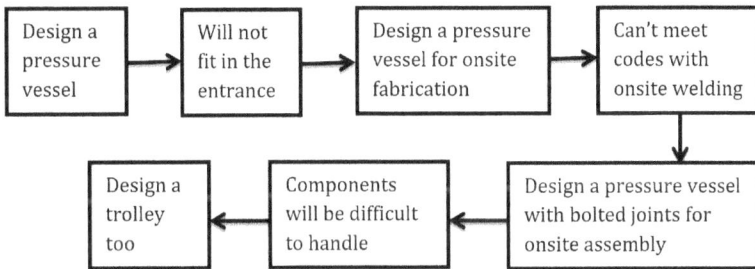

```
┌──────────┐    ┌──────────┐    ┌──────────────┐    ┌──────────────┐
│ Design a │    │ Will not │    │ Design a     │    │ Can't meet   │
│ pressure │───▶│ fit in the│──▶│ pressure     │───▶│ codes with   │
│ vessel   │    │ entrance │    │ vessel for onsite │    │ onsite welding│
└──────────┘    └──────────┘    │ fabrication  │    └──────────────┘
                                └──────────────┘           │
                                                           ▼
        ┌──────────┐    ┌──────────────┐    ┌──────────────────────┐
        │ Design a │    │ Components   │    │ Design a pressure vessel │
        │ trolley  │◀───│ will be difficult│◀─│ with bolted joints for │
        │ too      │    │ to handle    │    │ onsite assembly        │
        └──────────┘    └──────────────┘    └──────────────────────┘
```

An example of how problems can present as solutions are put forward (coevolution)

Normally, the problems engineers face are not fully defined. This means that as an engineer you will need to work out the full nature of the problem. However, simply researching and then researching some more can take time and you will probably never get a full picture of the problem you face. This is a common trap for younger engineers. They will sometimes think that they do not have the required information, that they can't solve the problem, and then decide to do nothing. This is probably more detrimental than researching too much – at least researching will teach you something.

A better way to understand such problems is to try solving them. By trying to solve them, you learn more about them as potential solutions fail, and you then better understand the problem to be solved. This process of solving the problem to better understand it is what's known as coevolution.

You can think of coevolution as the exploration of the design space. As you try new solutions you are exploring new areas of the possible solution – the design space. This tells you more about the nature of the problem, such as its boundaries. Eventually, through this continued exploration, you discover the area within the design space that correlates to a suitable solution or maybe even the best solution. The question you need to ask yourself is: Have I explored all of the areas I can or should explore?

Coevolution and experience

One of the reasons why engineers who have a lot of experience in one area can always work out the best solution is that they have done so much coevolving in the past. They now know almost all aspects of a technology, industry, product type etc. They can seem unfair when they dismiss a new idea. We can then think that they are conservative, uncreative or lazy. Chances are, they now just simply understand what the real problem is. This is not to say that an experienced engineer will always correctly dismiss a good new idea. It's simply a way to help understand how experience works in engineering.

If you are an experienced engineer, then realise that others may not have the benefit of your insights that have come from years of coevolving.

If you know an experienced engineer who has done a lot of coevolving, then treat them like a virtual lab. Test ideas with them and drill down to understand why they think the idea is good or not. You can learn from their experience coevolving.

2.2.4 Fixation

Have you ever needed to design something and noticed that your design looks a lot like designs by others? Or, have you seen someone come up with a really unique idea because they had never seen anything done by others before?

These are the result of fixation - or lack of.

When we see a solution that works, it can be hard to break away from it and come up with something new. This is not necessarily a bad thing. It obviously shows the potential to speed things up. More so, the solution that you're fixated on might actually be an optimum solution, and efforts to deviate from it will simply result in a poorer design or wasted effort.

However, at times we need to be unique. I have had students in FSAE (a competition run by the Society of Automotive Engineers for students who design, build and race an open-wheeled car) who have noticed this phenomenon. This proved detrimental when they needed to explain and justify their design on the day of the competition. Simply saying 'it worked last year' was insufficient; they needed a proper understanding of the design. Therefore, the students introduced a rule that when designing a component, they could not have the previous year's design in sight. This limited the fixation.

Given that fixation has advantages and disadvantages, you need to be aware of it and then decide if it will serve you well or if you need to take action to avoid it.

What's more, you need to be aware of fixating on your own ideas – sometimes called 'attachment'. At times it is best to stick with your initial idea. At other times, it is best to discard initial ideas after these have helped you understand the design space so that you can develop an improved solution. Once again, you need to be aware of fixation and decide what you will or should do.

2.2.5 Structured processes for solving problems

Should you use a structured process to solve your problems? Or should you be less constraining, and allow for a free flow towards the solution? Unfortunately, there is research suggesting each approach can be viable. Therefore, I can't give you a simple answer to this question.

Nevertheless, there is an acceptance in the research that there should be a general tendency toward a narrowing of the solutions allowed and there are usually a few clear phases at least (even if there is a little back tracking sometimes). However, the number of steps and the resolution of one step from the rest cannot be specified for all engineering problems. Instead, you need to be aware the problem you're solving, how well defined it is, where you feel you are with regards to solving it and what steps you think should be taken next – and perhaps after that – as you consider your strategy.

This can be extended to a higher level. However, I will not be covering the numerous design processes that have been covered in other texts. I will not be covering the many generic problem solving procedures that are covered elsewhere either. These are all reasonably easy to find. What I will say is that to get the best out of these processes, you need to do more than simply know what they are. You need to think about the kinds of problems that each process was intended to solve and determine if the process is likely to help you with what you are working on.

By thinking about the suitability of a strategy to a problem, you gain a better understanding of when and how a structured process can best help you.

2.2.6 Opportunism

Sometimes when you're working as an engineer, you will see an opportunity to use something that you know, an established piece of technology or an existing resource. By taking advantage of this opportunity, you are closer to solving the problem. It also often simplifies the problem – you now need to simply work at applying this resource or knowledge.

This is opportunism.

It is neither good nor bad; it depends upon how it is used. Thus, it is basically something you want to be aware of. Maybe it has genuinely made things easier. Or maybe it was easier, but the outcome was not so good.

Just watch yourself and others to see this play out. Try to understand if you use it as well as you could. You will be better at identifying when you are being opportunistic (or could be) and whether it is wise to be so given the situation.

2.2.7 Modal shifting

Problem-solving, as should be clear now, is not always a linear thing in engineering. The process of coevolution will require you to first try something (physically, in your mind, through drawing or via some other kind of simulation) think about what happened, re-examine the problem, and then try something new.

You will likely need to shift modes within the above steps as you consider any subproblem and then think about the overall problem and how the two relate. You might also need to think about how you will create a certain shape in CAD, and then actually create it, so that you can think about the implications of the proposed solution. Each of these tasks (or modes) is different, and moving from one to the other is a modal shift – especially when the thought process that goes with each mode is also different.

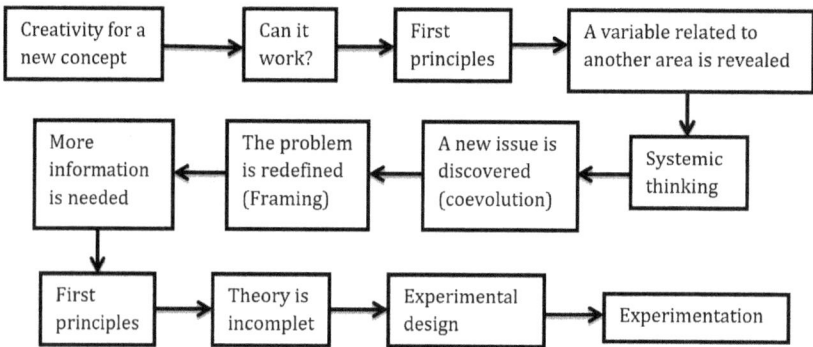

An example of the types of modal shifts an engineer could go through on a project

Research has shown that there are different types of modal shifts. It has also shown that success can be had when you can shift modes quickly and know what mode is needed. A common challenge faced by engineering students is working out whether they should be generating new ideas, finding out about established technology, applying theory or doing something else. This inability can result in people re-inventing or re-discovering "new" ideas. Or simply getting stuck because they can't find any information about what they should do next.

Having the ability to not get wrapped up in a specific task you are working on (as if it is the ultimate goal by itself), and remembering what you're ultimately trying to achieve (the real goal), will help make you a better engineer. Being able to quickly identify the mode you should be working in and shifting to the mode quickly will make you even better.

An anecdote from a colleague

An engineer who was recently an academic started to work for a company that made ozone generators – my colleague was his supervisor in this new role. He had been given a job and had studiously started working on it. Being an academic, he was skilled in applying first principles. However, he discovered a problem. His calculation results differed from the prototype performance measurement after four significant figures. He must have missed something! But what? The next two weeks were spent trying to resolve this discrepancy. When my colleague dropped by to see how it was all going, the engineer explained his trouble. There was a moment of silence with a certain facial expression on the face of my colleague. That was enough for the engineer to realise what he'd done, and go through a modal shift so that he could continue on with finding a solution to the problem he'd been given. Two weeks is a long time for a modal shift, but the engineer had probably gone through quite a few modal shifts while trying to get those extra significant figures agreeing: checking arithmetic, thinking about other phenomena at play, checking the measurement equipment. However, none of these were the modal shift that was needed – instead, he needed to shift into evaluation mode to determine if his model was good enough to progress to the next stage. Luckily for the engineer, my colleague forgives the first mistake – as long as it becomes a lesson. The lesson here is to take a step back and review what you're working on within the

context of what you need to get done. You might need
to shift modes.

Modal shifting, when it occurs, is often pre-empted by a realisation
that the current task is not progressing as desired or that it is about
to lead to an undesirable outcome. You will often feel it present
as a sense of confusion or a loss of direction. The key is to sense
this early – some people have to spend considerable time working
non-productively before they realise that they need to be doing
something different if they wish to progress.

Consider now if you are the kind of engineer who frequently realises
that they have been spending too much time on a task before they
change to another mode, or if you can pre-empt when it is time to
shift modes and do so. It is a type of meta-cognition – where you
monitor your thinking and decide what kind of thinking is needed
at that time.

2.2.8 Creativity

Many of us always assume that creativity is important. Some of
us say that, as engineers, we should be creative. Others say engineers shouldn't be creative. The biggest issue is that we do not
always agree on what creativity is. I stated in chapter 1 that creativity is part of being ingenious, and thus essential to being an
engineer. Therefore, I would certainly argue that engineers should
be creative.

Once again, I am going to use etymology to help understand what
exactly we should do when it comes to creativity to be better
engineers.

The word 'creative' can be traced back to the Latin *creatus*, meaning to 'make or bring forth'. It is related to words meaning to grow
or emerge. However, typically when we think of creativity, we think
of 'ideas'. If we combine these two meanings, then we can say

that creativity is the generation of ideas. The more creative you are, the more ideas you have. If you have many ideas, then it is more likely that you will have one that is good, or better, or even optimal. This is the adage that I have lived by when it comes to creativity in engineering.

I will talk more about creativity in chapter 5 , but mainly from an engineering perspective and the issues that engineers especially can have with creativity. For now though it is good to note two things:

- There seem to be elements of creativity within framing; the more ideas you have, the more frames you can have. Try generating a few frames for each problem you encounter.
- Creativity could also be the result of coevolution; as you explore the problem and better understand it, you can gain an understanding that allows a solution to be discovered (or created?).

Therefore, other practices can produce an effect similar to creativity or perhaps help to develop it. Use them to be more creative as well as for the intended purpose. In his book, *Engineering and the Mind's Eye*, Eugene S. Ferguson points out that a lot of engineering is a re-arrangement of established technology, and what will help an engineer more is direct and applied experience with technology. This will give you the insights into technology that can be later called upon while working as an engineer.

2.2.9 Sketching and seeing what is being thought

If you have ever seen *The Ghost and the Darkness*, (a movie released in 1996), then you might have noticed the scene where the engineer is designing a bridge. The movie is set more than 100 years ago, likely before standardised technical drawing had been fully formalised and adopted. The drawing that the engineer creates of the bridge is just that: a drawing.

At first glance anyone can see what it is. It is possible that the producer took liberties to make the movie more enjoyable for the layperson watching. However, it does indicate that engineers used to be better at communicating their ideas by sketch, which does indeed seem to be the case. It is certainly rare now, but I do occasionally come across engineering firms that send graduate engineers out to drawing classes so that they can better express their ideas through drawing.

Why is this?

As I mentioned above, it was easy for the layperson to see what the engineer had in his head – a bridge. This is the key to sketching that has been found many times when researching practices within technical professions. An ability to sketch allows one to communicate their ideas to others with incredible ease.

However, it does more than that. Sometimes drawing will let you better understand what you are thinking. Sometimes it reveals why an idea will not work and sometimes it reveals other ideas and possibilities. Other times it allows you to better understand the problem you are working on. It is good to be able to draw diagrams and such to understand systems, but creating an easy to understand visual representation of what is in your head is often the real need.

Think about how often your work could benefit from this skill and how well-developed this skill is in you. And note that you can always become better at it.

2.2.10 Scientific engineering versus science
Much of what I have written above is related to engineering from a design perspective. The comparison of engineers to other designers is often an interesting way of better understanding what makes

an engineer an engineer. However, another comparison, which might seem more obvious to you, is the comparison between engineering and science.

One quote I heard long ago that was intended to explain the differences between engineers and scientists was: *Scientists do the work of God; engineers do the work of humanity.*

The point being made here is that scientists try to better understand the world that we have – that is why they were once called natural philosophers. Engineers, on the other hand, simply look for ways of making the world a better place for people to live.

This would fit with the notion put forward by some that scientists discover scientific principles and engineers then apply these principles. However, this rules out advances in our scientific knowledge that have come from advances in technology. It also excludes the scientific work that engineers have had to do in the past to be able to achieve what they have achieved.

While two different fields, engineers will sometimes find themselves working as scientists and vice versa. Nevertheless, there is one big difference between the two that is well explained by the above quote. While scientists want knowledge to better understand the world, and always work towards gaining it; engineers need knowledge now so that they can solve the problem at hand. This difference in the purpose of knowledge leads to two interesting differences between engineers and scientists. Understanding these allows you to better understand what it is to be an engineer, which is essential to be a global engineer.

Engineer		Scientist
How to....?	The type of knowledge desired	Why does....?
Focus on a solution	Methods to solve the problem	Problem formulation
Improvement	Goal	Understanding

An indication of the differences between engineers and scientists. It is not a perfect comparison – there can be overlap – but it does help one understand the two roles

Setting boundaries on what you think about

This was brought to my attention when reading *What Engineers Know and How They Know It* by Walter Vincenti. If you were to read a textbook on thermodynamics for science students and one on the same topic for engineering students, then you would notice that in the engineering text, the author frequently puts an imaginary boundary around a system being considered. This does not happen in the science text. This is because scientists are only interested in the most basic of explanations about why things are the way they are. Engineers on the other hand, while liking the idea of knowing why things are the way they are, need to push on, even if they do not know all the 'whys'.

To accommodate the need to push on, sometimes a boundary can be set up so that only the balance of what passes the boundary needs to be considered. The fine details of what goes on within can be ignored. This technique can be used by engineers to simplify a problem, and let them continue when the specific scientific knowledge is as yet unavailable.

This approach can be useful for first principles. But whenever you have a problem that seems overly complicated, consider changing the boundary that you're using. This might simplify the challenge: allowing you to move on and start making decisions. What you would like to know and what you need to know are sometimes different.

Some examples to ponder

- Kanban: for those familiar with lean manufacturing, you know what this is. For others, Kanban is a system for managing the delivery of materials in production. Instead of trying to predict demand or precisely control all operations, which is very difficult even if it does provide a complete understanding of what is going on, the supply of materials is delivered when it is noticed that the reserves of those materials have become low. The boundary is placed around that one area of production and the flow in and out is observed.

- Public lavatories: have you ever washed your hands and then had to wait for the handdryer? Or maybe even waited to wash your hands? Perhaps waited for a cubicle, found a basin, but then had to wait for the dryer? Most lavatories seem to be designed with aesthetics or layout in mind. If one were to put conceptual boundaries around each step (cubicle, basin and dryer) and then determine the time taken for each step (thus getting the respective throughputs), then it would be possible to match the number of each to allow for a steady throughput and minimal waiting.

- Heating ventilation and air conditioning (HVAC): this is well known to many mechanical and civil engineers. The laws that govern this technology make up our understanding of the dynamics and thermodynamics of compressible fluid flow. This is not an area of scientific investigation that is easy. To this day, many aspects remain not fully understood. However, by focusing on the principles of conservation – what flows in, must eventually flow out – it is still possible to size heaters, pumps and air conditioning units.

Deriving formulae

We often express theory as a formula. Any formula has come from the derivation after making an assumption (a theory) about how the world works. If the formula agrees with experimental results, then the theory is not yet rejected, but instead, tested again. This is the scientific approach.

However, there is another source of formulae that scientists often know little about and, I have been told, often can't understand the need for.

Hopefully, you have done dimensional analysis when studying to be an engineer. However, like many, you might think that it is only for fluid mechanics. Fluid mechanics, due to its complex nature, is an ideal application for dimensional analysis. However, dimensional analysis is actually one of the most unique engineering things you can do. It is used when we want the accuracy and precision of a scientific formula, but lack the scientific knowledge.

Because dimensional analysis relies on the need to balance dimensions (or units depending upon what you were taught), it allows us to put greater structure around our tests and actually make enough sense of these so that you have something very close to a theoretically based formula without the known theory. When you start running tests to better understand a system that you're working on, do you simply run a large number of experiments and collect the data (hoping it makes sense) or do you take advantage of this uniquely engineering technique to be able to provide greater depth of understanding? Dimensional analysis is certainly something that all engineers should be aware of and use when appropriate.

An anecdote - why engineers should know and use dimensional analysis

The best book I have ever read on dimensional analysis is the work by Thomas Szirtes. In the preface, he explains how he came to discover dimensional analysis. I will not retell the whole story here – that would be too long. The essence was that, as a young engineer, Thomas was asked to analyse the deformation and force characteristics of a very large and complex antenna, which had not yet been made, for a number of loading conditions. It is often the tricky problems that are given to graduates in some companies. Because of the complexity, it was impossible to approach the problem analytically. This was also before numerical simulation methods were commonplace. Thomas was stuck. In desperation, he went to the library looking for something to help, but not knowing what to look for. You might recall what I said earlier about engineers needing to remember as much of what they learn as possible. Luckily, Thomas found a book on dimensional analysis. With the contents of the book, he was able to make a small model of the antenna, load it and then formulate the forces and deflections expected in the larger system. When he presented his findings, the in-house client was so impressed Thomas was was promoted to Engineering Specialist. Since then, Thomas has found that dimensional analysis has always helped quickly and with little effort – especially when other approaches had failed. When nothing else seems to work, the engineer can almost always fall back on dimensional analysis.

2.2.11 What is theory?

Have you ever heard people say that the theory works well in the lab, but not in the real world? Maybe people have suggested that theory only works in books. And yet, people are highly regarded when they find new theories. Why would we hold people in such high regard if what they have found doesn't actually work? Do we really think that Newton's laws of motion are wrong?

Is theory right or not?

Not many people realise this, but every theory you were taught is wrong.

I was lucky to have had a high school science teacher who took the time to explain how science works. Basically, it goes as follows:

1. Come up with an idea about how something in the world works (this could be done in any number of ways).
2. Think about the implications of this (this is often done mathematically, but not necessarily).
3. Devise an experiment that will test these implications.
4. Run the experiment.
5. Ask: Do the results of the experiment agree with the implications of the theory?
6. If the results agree, then the theory has passed the first test.
7. Now come up with another test for the theory.
8. If the results do not agree, create a new theory and start again.

The above method can be applied forever. You do not prove a theory; you disprove it. If a theory keeps on passing, then it has a better probability of being right. But it is only a probability. Never trust anyone who says something has been scientifically proven.

But does this really mean that when theory doesn't work for you, that you have disproved it? Do you really believe that you have found something new that no-one — none of all those people researching the respective area — has found? Probably not.

Often what happens is that people don't think properly about how they have applied the theory. However, we sometimes do not want to admit that we made a mistake. Instead, we decide to simply say that theory doesn't work in the real practical world where we live.

This attitude might make you feel better, but it will not make you a better engineer. Having the ego to be objective and admit that you have done something wrong can be a great help when you apply first principles.

An anecdote – using theory correctly

Sometime before writing this book, I was working in an R&D department. One of my colleagues was developing a small pressure relief valve. During preliminary tests, it was found that the pressure at which the valve seemed to open was much lower than what was expected. There was nothing compli- cated about the valve; it was basically a flat disc pushed onto the sealing surface by a spring, with an O-ring in between the surface and the disc.

The pressure should have equalled the force from the spring compression divided by the area inside the O-ring. My col- league double-checked the spring design, the compression of the spring and the diameter of the O-ring — pretty much everything he thought was affecting the release pressure. He went over the calculations again and again. Everything looked right, but the measurements with calibrated equipment told a different story.

If this were a more complex system, then dismissal of the theory might have been likely. However, no-one was going to suggest that the basic formulae for pressure and force or Hooke's law were wrong. The fact that the principles at play were so fundamental and trusted made everyone think more deeply about the issue.

It was eventually found that the parts being used were not sufficiently flat and smooth (this was a prototype; not a production unit). This meant that to seal, first the pressure to be sealed against had to be overcome and then the O-ring needed to be compressed enough so that it would fill the small dips in the sealing surfaces. Remember how I said it was a small valve? In a large valve, the area multiplied by pressure would be much larger than in a small valve. However, the force to compress the O-ring would not be that different. Thus, the effects of the O-ring compression were much more significant in the smaller seal.

This realisation came after a reasonable period, and shows that we can get stuck with a certain perspective that limits our ability to work out what is going on (note the creative blocks covered later). Up until that time, no-one in the department had worked on such small valves, and the effects of surface roughness when working with prototypes had never been something we had to take into account.

When you find a difference between your results and your predictions, think about your equivalent of a rough surface that you might have ignored. We sometimes assume the world is too perfect, and then blame the theory.

2.3 Chapter summary

Chapter 2 has explained to you what makes for an excellent engineer (framing, systemic thinking and first principles) that is independent of any specific culture or context. That is a global engineer. It also covered a number of the aspects of engineering design that you can use to augment your engineering ability.

It is wise for you to now consider which you are most in need of improving.

Next, we need to talk about how you will improve those attributes so that you too are a global engineer. Make sure you are familiar with the content of this chapter so you are ready for what comes next.

3.

Improving your Engineering Ability

I have gone over the basics of thinking and cognition that are unique to engineering. This is not to say that these unique aspects of engineering make up the totality of what engineering is. Engineers, like all professionals, need to master time management, develop their interpersonal skills, negotiate with others to find solutions that are good for the company, navigate the politics of the workplace, have excellent communication skills and so on.

There are many books and other resources that will help you develop these skills. They are skills that you should continually develop throughout your career, and I would encourage you to always be mindful of them and their improvement. However, these are not the skills that I am focusing on in this book.

This book focuses on those skills that make an engineer different from other professionals. Before you can start improving your engineering skills, it is wise to think about your current level of expertise.

3.1 Your expertise now

A note for students: You might be an engineering student or you might be thinking about becoming an engineering student. Depending upon your level of education, it will be harder to properly evaluate the current level of your engineering skills. This is particularly so when you are thinking about your skills in applying first principles. However, systemic thinking and

47

framing are more universal. For this reason, I will link abilities in these skills to more general characteristics so that you can better understand what you should work on to improve your engineering ability.

3.1.1 First principles

There are two aspects to using first principles. The first is seeing them in the world around you. The second is working out how to apply them.

When you learn about scientific theory, do you easily see it in action in various contexts? Or, do you tend to think of it as something you simply need to learn, but it is different from the 'real world'? If you do not see scientific theory in action in various aspects of your daily life, then you do have some work to do - start looking for them in everyday events.

Do you prefer to investigate options or do you prefer to have a procedure to follow? 'Options people' will like the idea of taking a different way home from work to investigate the possibility of finding a better way. 'Procedural people' will always want to take the same way home. The paradox is that procedural people will often do well in an engineering course when they learn engineering sciences (the first principles), but the application of first principles requires an investigation of options.

Therefore, if you're a procedures person, you will likely do well in engineering studies – you will be able to master the procedures that will enable you to answer the exam questions in those engineering science subjects. However, you might feel frustrated applying the theory to a real-world application because typically it will not be as 'clean' as an exam question, and you will need to try a few options before finding the best way to apply theory to the problem. If you are a more procedures-based person, then you will likely have to take action to improve your ability to apply first principles.

There is however a lesson in this for all us. Something I seem to frequently need to learn again and again. You can't expect to always know all of the principles at play. Sometimes, you will need to do some research. Usually, you will at least know the discipline that likely holds the principles that you need. However, at times you might not even know that. This is no excuse to ignore first principles. Instead, it is a chance to learn more. You just need to put some effort into finding the right resources. This is when having a network of other engineers and technical people in various industries (and even some academics) is ideal. When I was working in the water products industry, for example, it was handy knowing a corrosion chemist.

3.1.2 Framing

To recap, framing is basically taking a problem as it is presented to you and then turning it into a problem to be solved by someone with engineering skills. This requires both creativity and a willingness to confront problems. Everyone could be a bit more creative, but if you feel this is not your strong point, then it's something that you will need to work on to be able to frame well, and be a better engineer. Secondly, you will also need to be proactive in redefining any problem as it is presented to you.

If you think any of the following describe you, then you probably need to work on your framing ability:

- You consider yourself more reactionary.
- You would rather be told exactly the problem to be solved.
- You would rather be told how to solve a problem.
- You have trouble working out where to begin. This is a common one if you were taught in a procedural manner, which is more frequent in engineering degrees than is desirable.

3.1.3 Systemic thinking

Do you think you're a big-picture thinker or a detailed thinker? Detailed thinkers tend to dive straight into a problem and start working on it. If you are a detailed thinker, then this can cause you to start working on the wrong problem. It can also mean that you might make decisions without thinking about their broader consequences. Thus, if you are more inclined to be a detailed thinker, then you will need to work on improving your systemic thinking ability.

3.2 Improving your engineering abilities

Now that you have an idea of what you need to work on to become an excellent engineer, I am going to share with you how you can indeed become an excellent engineer.

3.2.1 Preparing for change

Before I talk about specific tasks that you can use to become a better engineer, I want to delve into the nature of change required.

You will need to change the way you think. Engineering is an intellectual task (it is all about thinking), and thus you can't improve without changing the way you think. Sometimes, we feel that we are giving up part of ourselves if we change the way we choose to think about things. You might even find that some of what I have written conflicts with your beliefs about what engineering is, and this can cause a sense that you need to change your beliefs. Changing either your thinking or your beliefs can feel like you are losing something. While you will indeed need to change to improve, you should not feel that you are losing something. Because, you are instead enhancing your abilities and becoming more balanced.

In chapter 6, I am going to talk about how your background can affect your ability to be a fully competent engineer who can work anywhere in the world – a global engineer. However, for now it is worth noting that as each of us matures we tend to naturally find a balance. This is because we work on strengthening our own various weaknesses as we notice them (consciously or unconsciously). Therefore, much of what I am going to cover is actually a collection techniques to accelerate this natural maturity that would come from years of working as an engineer. So you can improve your engineering ability as quickly as possible. Thinking of this as accelerated development, might be more acceptable than thinking of it as change.

3.2.2 The nature of expertise

Do you think engineering expertise is innate (almost genetic) or something that can be developed with practice?

Research into expertise and what allows one to become an expert can be traced back to the work of Sir Francis Galton in 1869. Sir Francis found that people within England who had demonstrated remarkability within their chosen field were typically closely related to others who had also shown remarkability within their chosen field (though not necessarily the same field). This led Sir Francis to surmise that there was some inheritable characteristic that allowed people to become brilliant within the area they had chosen.

This might make you think you need to have a genetic disposition towards developing the characteristics that will make you an expert engineer.

However, more recent research into expertise actually found that the key to expertise, in general, is simple: practise!

We often think that people are 'naturals'. You might even sometimes be tempted to use this as an excuse for not being as skilled at something as you would like to be. However, most people who seem to have a 'natural ability' have actually had years of practise. They either do not tell people about this practise because it helps with the mystery that they must maintain – this is especially true of entertainers – or they simply engaged in related practise from an early age because of enjoyment – this is more common of athletes and sportspeople. This has been found to be true of activities as diverse as comedy, athletics, chess, dance and mathematics. The area you wish to be an expert in is unimportant; what is important is the practise that you engage in. It must be deliberate practise.

Any task used for deliberate practice will have the following characteristics:

- It's designed specifically to improve performance.
- It can be repeated numerous times.
- Feedback on results is continuously available.
- It's highly demanding mentally.
- It isn't much fun – hopefully, you will enjoy aspects of it, but it's often the aspects that are not fun that separate the novice from the expert.

The last point is obviously subjective in nature; however, it reiterates that the goal of deliberate practice is to develop a set attribute. It is not simply doing the general task again and again and hoping that you become better at it. You drill those things that need to be drilled to ensure that you have all the attributes required for expertise. This might be what separates you from other engineers. If you take the time to develop key attributes to become a better engineer while others do not, then you will become the better engineer.

The tasks that I will cover soon have been found, either by me or others, to be ideal deliberate practice for the development of engineering expertise. They are based on general types of practise tasks that have been found to be suitable for the development of professional expertise.

The flipside of deliberate practise – and being a global engineer

Just as deliberate practise can make you better at something, it can also make you unsuitable. The reason why background does affect engineering design ability is that you have spent most of your life in one area (cultural, economic, national, organisational etc.). By doing this, you are naturally engaging in deliberate type practise as you get better at performing the tasks your environment demands. Then, when there is a change in your environment (from you relocating or your company changing for example), you will find that there are new skills (skills you might not have developed) that are required.

By ensuring that you develop skills that are at the core of excellent engineering, you will be universal enough to work as an excellent engineer anywhere, and be a global engineer.

3.2.3 Improving your first principles ability

The best way to improve your ability to use first principles is to also develop your ability to model. In this case, I mean creating an analytical model of whatever system you are dealing with. For many engineers, this can be difficult because they are so accustomed to calculating instead of modelling. However, if you put the effort into creating an algebraic model of each system you are working on, then you will see a steady improvement in your understanding of first principles and how to use them.

This likely sounds good, but there is a definite chance that it also sounds like something that is beyond you. What confuses most engineers is where to begin. So let's consider how you can get started.

Why? Why? Why?

One reason why some engineers have trouble with first principles is that they are interested in how something works. 'How?' is a good question. However, it is sometimes superficial when com-pared to the question 'why?' How many times have you looked at an engineering system and asked why it works, rather than how it works? Asking only 'how?', gives you enough understanding to feel comfortable with a system and potentially diagnose faults. Asking 'why?' forces you to think more deeply and apply theory to whatever system you're considering. Once you have identi-fied the theories (first principles), you then need to bring them together so that you have a model that you can use to evaluate and optimize.

One of the best techniques that I have come across to help engi-neers develop their modelling ability and the application of theory is the fishbone diagram (also called the 'Ishikawa diagram'). If you're not familiar with this diagram, then a basic one is shown below.

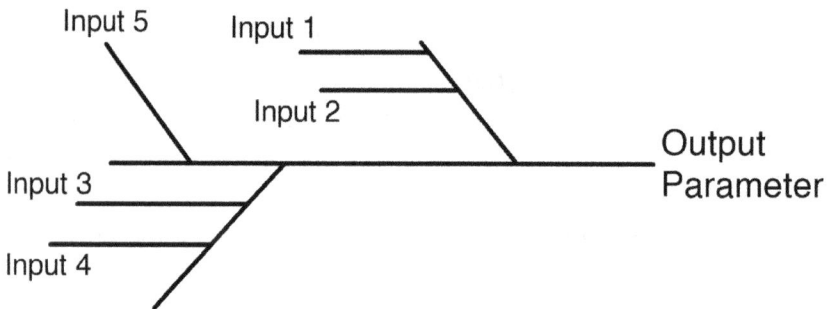

Drawing out the mathematical/theoretical relationships between the output and inputs in a diagram can be an excellent way to work out which first principles need to be applied and how – it's an excellent starting point

The main horizontal line represents the main parameter you are interested in. This might be the temperature of a heater, the strength of a support beam or maybe the speed of an electric motor.

The branches coming out of the horizontal line represent the parameters and variables that directly affect the output: current, resistance, width, length, voltage etc. The branches from these first branches represent the variables and parameters that affect the variables and parameters of the first branches. You continue to add branches until the last branches added represent the variables that you can set. On occasion, I have found multiple branches have the same inputs. You might find that, as you add more variables, you need to change the fishbone diagram into something more complicated. That's fine – don't let a tool, that is somewhat arbitrary, constrain your application of first principles or distort the accurate presentation of what you are analysing.

Once you have completed the diagram, you replace each branch with a mathematical expression. For example, the output might be spring force f, and two branches from it would make up stiffness k and compression x. This would be replaced with $f = k\,x$. Note, that this is an algebraic expression and not a calculation. You will then have a complete model that you can use to investigate, understand and optimize the system you are working on.

I have made the above explanation sound rather simple, but it can be difficult. To make it easier, there are three important things to keep in mind when creating a model:

1. It can take a few attempts. Do not expect the first model to be correct. Sometimes you need to take a few goes, leave it for a period and then come back to it. This is the art side of modelling.
2. You need to make sure that you have identified the right output variable before starting. Typically, this is a failure mode that you are worried about or the characteristic that defines the purpose of the system. Each system might have a few failure modes and a few purposes so you might

need to generate a few models depending upon what you need to do.

3. Know how sophisticated and accurate the model really needs to be. Sometimes engineers think they need to consider everything or else nothing has been properly considered. However, it could be that the analysis of a simplified version of the system in question is enough. If you're estimating the thermal load when designing a cooling system for a hen house, then maybe treating each hen as a spherical chicken radiating energy at body temperature is good enough for the model.

Even with the above, the application of first principles can be confronting. The only way you can become better at it is to actually try it. Make the decision now to start using first principles by modelling the systems you are working on. Think about what you are working on now. How would you start modelling it?

This could also mean changing your attitude towards theory (recall the discussion on theory earlier). From now on, you do not want to engineer systems that will get the job done. You want all the engineering systems that you are responsible for to be optimum. You want to know that, given the constraints and resources available, this is the best that can be done. You can only achieve this (and be sure you have achieved this) by using theory. Once you make a commitment to ensuring everything is optimum, your interest and motivation in applying first principles will flow naturally as a matter of course.

Is it testing or validating?

Some people have trouble viewing theory as something useful. They compartmentalise it in their mind as something that they need to learn and apply in an exam, but not something that can be used practically. Then, when it comes time to take on real challenges, they resort to other methods: like guessing, trial and error, and repeating what was done before. There is nothing ingenious about this, and it should not be viewed as the proper practice of an engineer.

I am again reminded of the saying that an engineer uses only 5% of their education. I hear it most from mediocre engineers. They might be successful, and they might get promoted to managerial positions because they are good at running projects, but I have never met a great engineer with this attitude.

I have also noticed something else common to mediocre engineers. They talk more about testing than validating. I did not notice this until I was talking with a colleague from General Motors about Formula SAE (Formula Student, in other parts of the world). I had asked him to be part of a team of engineers to review the design my students were working on – it's always good to get practising engineers to help out with this because, for some reason, students never listen to their lecturers. He made the observation that students in these programs can often confuse testing and validating. They design something and then test the design — much like an exam. However, the attitude should be that they are validating their design decisions. They should be so confident in each decision that they should be validating that all has been done correctly, and no errors are expected.

If you take this attitude (validating ideas, and not testing them) when designing your next engineering artefact, then you will automatically take first principles more seriously. Try this from now on.

I should point out here that, sometimes, you do need to test. I had to do this when working on an electrified aerial vehicle. The suppliers of the propeller and the motor had insufficient data so I needed to generate it myself. This is different – this is gaining data to let you design, which is not testing your design. Make sure that any testing you do do, really needs doing.

Even if you're motivated, and even if you have a good framework for the model that needs to be made, you sometimes just get stuck. In these cases, you need a tool to get further insights.

What if ...?

A tool that I have used to help engineering students when applying first principles is to ask 'what if...?' Usually, you make these questions extreme. Some examples are:

- What if this part were made of foam? This was to help students create a model for the deflection of parts in a bolted joint. By imagining that one part was more compliant, they could better understand this deflection. Imagining one part being soft can often help us understand how a system works when parts are solid.

- What if the lever arm was 100 times longer? This question was used when trying to model a self-locking system based on a balance of moments.

- What happens if the force/current/flow/rotation/movement is reversed? This is a universal question that uses the failure of the item being modelled to understand its workings under proper conditions.

- What happens if the force/current/flow/rotation/movement is zero or infinite? Extremes are absolute, and easier to imagine. By understanding the conditions at the extremes, you can then work out what the nature of the mathematics should be. This can then trigger your unconscious mind to put forward an idea that will help.

Note these are just some examples. It is much easier to come up with questions when you are considering something specific. If you are looking for a general guide to using this approach, then go through each possible variable and ask what would happen if it were really low or really high in value. Use your engineering insight and experience to answer the question. If the change makes no difference, then the variable is not important. If the variable does make a difference, then use the insights of the difference you determined to work out what the mathematical relationship should be.

Sometimes when you ask 'what if?' questions, you know that they will help, but you can't answer them. In these instances, an analogy can help — especially an emotion-inducing one. Let's consider some examples now.

Make yourself a machine

A common issue engineers have when trying to apply first principles is determining what causes what. This becomes less common with experience, but inexperienced engineers, especially those who study to pass the exam as opposed to learn, can make mistakes like effectively assuming acceleration causes a force as opposed to the other way around.

One solution to this is to imagine you or part of your body is a part of the engineering artefact you are working on. One example that I have always noticed works well is when students imagine their head is inside a self-locking clamp. This always helps them draw a proper free-body diagram – the thought of a crushed skull just seems to activate more of the mind. Some need to physically grab their head and squeeze so do not be afraid to actually get physical with yourself if you use this method.

Other examples include:

- Imagine planking as a simply supported beam or a cantilever beam to determine the point of maximum stress.

- Imagine you are an electron radiating a magnetic field as you try to run through the tunnel of a copper wire. How will your magnetic field interact with another magnetic field if it is applied?

- Imagine you are a vapour molecule hitting the liquid surface and getting stuck as you knock a 'friend' molecule into the vapour by exchanging energy in a liquid vapour system.

- Imagine that you are the one turning machinery as opposed to a motor or engine. This is a handy way to work out reactionary forces (where you need to place your feet) so you can understand the reactionary torque, which can often cause confusion.

- Imagine you are on a roller coaster in the shape of a serpentine belt drive to understand the centrifugal effects as the belt runs over different pulleys in the system.

As a general rule, as you start to consider processes that get further from solid mechanics (towards systems such as flowing fluids and magnetic fields) the analogies with your body become more abstract. Nevertheless, they can help you develop your understanding of a system – even if it is just because it makes you look at the system from another perspective or triggers your emotions, and gets more of your brain working on the task. Give it a try whenever you are stuck trying to apply first principles.

How difficult are first principles?

I have worked with engineers from many parts of the world trying to apply first principles. It ranges from simply thinking to use them, to understanding the right ones for a given situation, to creating complex models of engineering systems, to combining such models with probability theory to predict quality (that's what my first research specialisation was in). In all these cases, I have found that the application of first principles is a challenge. I know I mentioned that this is harder earlier on, but it is worth noting now, that despite the fact that some cultures will have a greater appreciation for the value of first principles, I am yet to find one where the majority of engineers are adept at first principles. I have actually found that it seems to be more a function of desire than anything else. Some people like the idea of being able to predict behaviour and optimize, and this allows them to push past the initial difficulty to develop this attribute. The hardest thing to do is that which you dislike. Imagine the benefit of being good at first principles and the pleasure you could derive from predicting the behaviour of something you are working on. This will help you keep a positive mindset as you work on developing this attribute. And that will help you achieve this goal.

3.2.4 Improving your framing ability

Framing is a bit mysterious. Sometimes it's simply that ability to decide how to move forward and sometimes it's very creative – consider the example with Gordon Murray from earlier. What is the most important aspect of framing: the speed; the creativity of it; or the number of frames generated for consideration?

There is no clear knowledge about what makes for the best framing. But you have already been framing anyway. Each time you solve a problem, you have to decide how you will approach it or what the real problem is that you have to solve (or choose to solve). So we at least know what it is.

What is probably most important is your ability to create a frame that turns the stated problem into an engineering problem, and allows you to move forward with developing an engineering solution. The next most important thing is understanding the frame you have chosen and why you have chosen it – this will let you determine how to improve your framing ability. I will go into more detail about how your background can affect the way you frame and work as an engineer in general. However, if, for now, you consider how any frame you choose is affected by your experiences, then you will be better able to determine if it is the best frame, or if there might be a better one.

To improve your ability to understand how you frame, you can consider how other people frame. By understanding the various frames used by others, you can better think about what frames to use yourself. Whenever you read about a new engineering system, or see a program about it or hear about it from colleagues, try to reverse the design process. This will bring you back to the frame that those responsible for this system used. Once you have the frame that you think was used, think about what frame *you* might have used. Then consider why the frames are different. This will help you understand your own framing behaviour and make you think about how else you could frame. This will in turn expand your ability to generate a number of frames and decide which frame you should progress with.

Once you know how you frame and you become more aware of why you frame that way, you will become better at it. Therefore, just putting the effort into looking at new engineering systems and working out the respective frame will make you better at framing. However, to make the most of this, beware of the following:

- Stating the solution: sometimes we focus too much on the final solution as opposed to the essence of the solution that guided the engineer to find the solution.
- Restating the problem: at the other extreme, we use fancier words to describe the problem, or simply put words like

'engineer a system that solves' in front of the respective problem statement.

An example of framing mistakes

An example might help at this time. Consider the problem below and the different types of responses (frames) to it.

The problem requiring a frame:

In some parts of the world people are often placed under water restrictions from the mains supply, and would like to supplement their home water use with rainwater that they have collected in a tank. If there is no rainwater in the tank, then they still want to be able to use mains water. However, they want this to be easy to do (i.e. still use their existing taps) and water authorities are concerned that untreated water (including rainwater) will enter the mains system.

A frame that is actually a solution:

Supply all the home water from a rainwater tank and top it up with mains via an air break (air gap) system to ensure that no rainwater can get into the mains system. Then, use a pump to bring the water up to pressure when needed for use in the home.

A frame that restates the problem:

Develop a water management system that lets people easily use any stored rainwater and adheres to all local laws regarding the use of water.

An engineering frame:

Design a domestic scale water management system that connects to a home at the outlet and to mains and the rainwater at each of two inlets.

The first example requires very little engineering. The solution is basically there; a draftsman could draw something up or a plumber could implement it. There is no more need for being ingenious. However, the solution put forward has a frame and ingenuity within it. The frame was to treat the rainwater as a primary supply and view the mains as the supplement. This is a removal of the first frame and the application of a new one. While the statement hides the frame, it is still creative and ingenious. Nevertheless, the hiding of the frame within the solution also hides the thinking and framing that went into it.

The second frame sounds more like a formal statement from a marketing department to be given to the engineering department. It is more formal and states requirements concisely, but the engineer still needs to work out how they will approach (frame) the problem to solve it.

The third frame doesn't designate the specifics. A pump is probably going to be needed somewhere and a check valve of some sort will likely be needed to prevent backflow into the mains. However, the engineer now knows how they are going to move forward. They have turned the problem into an engineering problem: design a water management system. There is still room for more engineering (who knows what other challenges are to come), but a direction has been chosen and everyone on the team will know what they are working on.

As a closing on how to know what a frame is, it's a bit like this: If you came up with a frame on Friday at the end of the workday, then you would know exactly what engineering tasks you need to engage in first thing Monday morning. These engineering tasks might be: designing experiments, starting some CAD, calculating parameters, brainstorming about a specific challenge, selecting materials, looking through technical catalogues or something else that is clearly done by an engineer. You don't yet have the exact solution, but you know what you're working towards and you have a good idea about how you're going to get there. That's what a good framing ability offers you: direction.

Also, by understanding the frame you had, you can better understand how your perspective can affect your tendencies as an engineer. This can in turn help you frame better in the future and continue to improve as an engineer. Many engineers feel they keep making a basic mistake each time they take on a problem. They wonder why other engineers always seem to start off on the right path and they don't. However, they can't work this out. They simply haven't taken the time to understand how they framed and why they framed the way they did.

3.2.5 Improving your systemic thinking

Systemic thinking is usually well developed through experience. Most engineers have been caught out so many times after not considering the full system that they have learned to think systemically (think about as many related issues, aspects and items as possible) when developing an engineering solution. However, some engineers do not, and if you are a new engineer, then you will want to accelerate this so that you can quickly become an expert engineer.

Another reason why most experienced engineers would have developed good systemic thinking is that there is little substitute for it. First principles can be substituted (sort of) by experiment, trial and error or reverse engineering (perhaps a polite way of saying 'copying smarter people'). Framing only needs to be done once. And out of a group of people, only one person will need to come up with a frame (probably expressed as a solution, but still it gets the team moving). Framing too can be copied from others. However, systemic thinking needs to be applied each time a decision is made. If you do not think about the full system when making a decision, then it is likely something will go wrong.

It seems to me that the need for systemic thinking is what led to the common adoption of concurrent or simultaneous engineering. That is, all subsystems need to be developed concurrently. This includes the manufacturing system (if it is a product) the servicing system (if it is something that will need maintenance) and so on. This approach forces engineers to think about not just their subsystem, but the entire system, which can include everyone and everything that interacts with the system in some way – it's up to you to decide where the system boundaries are.

Nevertheless, there are some organizations where, due to the nature of the work or the philosophy of the management, concurrent engineering is not really practised. In these situations, if you want to improve your systemic thinking, you will need to take action yourself.

Here are two related things that you can do:

1. From now on, each time you need to make a decision, think about who else or what else is affected by it. Ask what you can do to make it easier for them, or what they could do to make your proposed solution better.

2. For larger projects, take the time to talk to as many affected people as possible at each stage. This is not easy, but it is effective. I have been in companies where my management could not understand why I was talking to workers on the factory line, people in the quality department, people in servicing and people in warranty. This actually had a slightly negative effect upon my manager's view of me – some people do think an engineer should sit alone and come up with the ideal solution single-handedly. However, the benefits of these conversations were remarkable:

a. After the conversations, I had collected a list of potential problems that I would avoid so that prototyping would run smoothly.

b. I also had identified a number of other requirements that would make the respective product cheaper to make, transport and service. You can imagine how a much more successful a product will be if it is easier to produce, distribute and service.

c. Finally, I had gained much more respect and appreciation from others in the organization. This allowed me to progress projects faster. It also meant that if there was an issue, then people would deal directly with me so that the issue too could be resolved faster.

From what I have experienced, there are two challenges that can make the above difficult — thinking about the big picture and being extroverted enough to talk to another person.

Some of us are naturally good at the big picture thinking and some of us are naturally good at the details. Stop and think now. Do you prefer to get into the finer points of a system and make sure that things are right? Or do you prefer to come up with a basic idea at the big picture level? Which is best for engineering?

Engineering actually needs both, and you need to be good at both. Fortunately, if you have a tendency for one, you can still develop the other. It's just handy to know which it is you need to develop. In the next section I will cover more about managing how you think, but for now, know that systemic thinking needs you to shift from the details, to the big picture and then back and forth. By working on this shifting, much like the modal shifting I mentioned earlier, you will become better at it.

I have worked with a few engineers who do find it hard to approach a new person and start talking to them about anything. If it is work-related, then it is a little easier, but if they are in another department, then that can add a perceived barrier that actually makes it harder.

Are you a more introverted person or an extroverted person? If it is the former, then you will need to take action to account for this. You do not need to sell yourself out, and change your personality. Instead, you might simply need to use methods that encourage interaction. You can write an email to the respective people, ask a colleague to organize a meeting of key people to share the ideas (you only need other perspectives not the human interaction) or you could set up an online forum that you invite people to. There are numerous ways to do this, just don't let your introverted nature hold back your ability to develop your systemic thinking and engineering ability. If you are an extrovert, then use a checklist – otherwise you might spend the whole meeting talking about the weekend instead of asking key questions.

3.2.6 Taking a broader perspective on your ability

In the previous sections, I have covered techniques that you can use to better yourself as an engineer by developing key traits that have been found in expert engineers. You will be able to apply theory correctly so that your solutions are optimum, you will be better able to work out what solution direction is best for a problem, and you will produce solutions that perform optimally on all fronts.

However, this expertise comes from three separate attributes. By understanding how to bring them together, you can amplify the benefits. You can gain even more benefit by then augmenting your expertise with an understanding of the cognitive processes covered in section 2.2. To bring this all together, you use a process called meta-cognition. In short, you think about how you should think.

Meta-cognition starts with an awareness of how you're thinking. Then you determine if it is the right way to think given the problem that you're working on. Finally, if you decide that there is a better way of thinking, then you shift to that mode of thinking. Once again, recall the modal shifting that I covered earlier.

In summary: once you are aware of the different ways that engineers think when solving problems and you develop those thinking skills, the next thing to do is combine this understanding of thinking with meta-cognition.

As I mentioned in the section on modal-shifting, meta-cognition can be hard. It doesn't come naturally to us to shift our thinking around. Students especially, when they are developing their ability to apply first principles within an engineering design project, often find it difficult to determine when they need to be creative, when they need to apply first principles and when they need to research established technology. This is based on my experience and research in developing engineering skills in students. Because it is naturally difficult to shift our cognition like this, we need tools to help us do this and improve our thinking.

The best tool I have come across for this purpose is the Six Hats system developed by Edward de Bono, who also developed the term 'lateral thinking'. I will not go over the whole system here. Instead, I will point out the essence of it, which can help with meta-cognition. I do encourage you to read his work though – see the references.

The essence of the Six Hats approach is determining the type of thinking that is ideal for a certain problem and the best order in which each type is applied. Each time you take on a new challenge, ask yourself what is required. Do you need to apply some first principles first to better understand the situation? Should you first think about the frame you want to use, and then think about what you will do next? (Note: you can decide to plan only some of the way and then think about what to do next, in case you feel that more understanding will be gained as you pursue the solution.) Perhaps you need to collect some specific information, which might include first principles, and then start thinking about a frame?

By taking this first step, you automatically engage in meta-cognition. And you can then expect to become better at the other types of thinking and bringing them together.

However, some people are not good at being given these options. I have worked with an engineer or two who just wanted to know what to do and start doing it. These engineers found it harder to work through the options because they just wanted a procedure to follow. On the other hand, there are engineers who like having options and enjoy creating a procedure to follow. But, the people who have the tendency towards dealing with options sometimes don't want to follow the procedures developed. This is a paradox: those who can create the procedure might not like to follow it and those who want a procedure to follow don't like having too many options to choose from so they can't create a procedure to follow.

Regardless of where you sit on the spectrum between wanting options and wanting a procedure, developing an ability to determine the best way to think about each engineering problem you encounter is probably the best way to become a global engineer. Everything in this book is essentially a guide. It is to help you manage your thinking as a global engineer — one who can find an engineering solution no matter where they are or what problem they face.

If you take one thing away from this book, it is that a global engineer will evaluate the challenge they face and then consider the best way to think about this challenge before they take action.

Put simply: They think about their thinking.

4.

Engineering Teams

I assume that you want to be the best engineer that you can be – that's why you're reading this book. You might also want to be a remarkable engineer. One that does something amazing. Something that people (or maybe only those in your industry) talk about for years to come. Let's consider this notion a little further before talking about teams - you will soon understand why I chose to do this here.

4.1 Heroic engineers from history

While they are not spoken about a lot in the popular media, there are famous engineers who are known for their individual contributions and achievements. Some of these engineers are:

- Isambard Kingdom Brunel – a mechanical and civil engineer who worked on many public works in England in the 19th century.
- J.J.C. Bradfield – sometimes called 'the father of Sydney Harbour Bridge' and sometimes called 'the father of modern Sydney'. He was a major contributor to the design of Sydney Harbour Bridge and managed much of the construction in the early 20th century. But still, he did work with others.

- Werner von Braun – an engineer who contributed much to the development of rocket technology during WWII and to the US space program. He was also known as an excellent manager and leader of other engineers.

- Corradino D'Ascanio – the engineer who designed the MP6 Vespa, which laid down the foundations, in the mid-1940s, for the Vespa designs still common today. The Vespa is a favourite example of mine because it was a design that had to accommodate low cost due to the war, durability due to poor roads, functionality for the mass market and it still managed to have style. Say what you will; I think the Vespa is a brilliant example of Italian engineering at its best. He also designed the first production helicopter.

- Howard Hughes – an engineer and businessman who, among other things, contributed to the shape of the air industry at the time.

- Thomas Telford – described by some as the 'man who built Britain'.

4.2 Where have the heroes gone?

We rarely hear about such people today. Some argue that engineers are simply not as highly regarded by society as they once were, and pine for such times. But the truth is that the majority of engineering projects are so complex that no one person can truly be responsible for them. This makes it much harder for the mainstream media to identify those singular 'heroic' engineers. The situation becomes even more evident when you consider the rate of globalisation. Not only are you now more likely to work with a team of engineers, but that team could very likely be international.

With typical engineering projects being so much more complex, they require teams of engineers. Therefore, if you wish to be an excellent engineer, you will need to work well with others. However, this is more than simply having good interpersonal skills.

Louis L. Bucciarelli in *Designing Engineers* explains it very well.

> *Moreover, in the contemporary engineering firm, designing engages more than a lone engineer at a drafting board or work station. The design of a photovoltaic module, or an x-ray inspection system, or a new paper handler for photoprint processor engages a wide variety of people within the firm: research scientist, marketing chief, lab technician, systems engineer, project manager, production engineer, purchasing agent, inventory controller. All can and do influence the design, and all must come to an agreement in order to realize the design. The process is thus social, the business of a subculture. Not surprisingly, participants' visions of the social process of designing are strongly influenced by their understanding of the way the things they are designing work. To participants in design, the object serves as a kind of icon that embodies a set of attitudes and ways of thinking that are peculiar to engineering.*

With the complex tasks that engineers work on, it becomes essential to ensure that you, and other engineers, share the same understanding of the technical requirements of the project and its ongoing state. Otherwise, the engineering team will not actually have the desired effect: A single 'super engineer' (made of multiple engineers in the team) that can work at a speed that is proportionally (numerically equal to the number of team members) faster than a single engineer.

4.3 The modern engineering entity (the team)

In effect, an engineering team should be akin to a single entity with many minds all aware of where a project is going, where it is at and what needs to be done. Furthermore, each part of the entity needs to be aware of what the other parts are doing. The essence of this state is referred to as having both shared cognition and shared situational awareness, which are both concepts developed in team theory. Ensuring this shared cognition is really the responsibility of the manager in any team or organization. However, you can take action yourself to ensure that you are as well-connected with your team as possible.

Always try to do the following:

- Say what you mean and mean what you say – an emphasis on communicating exact concepts removes interpretation and erroneous interpretation.

- Try to use numbers and other measures whenever possible – what you might think is a reasonable description, another might think is hyperbole (always try to avoid hyperbole and euphemisms). This is not possible with numbers.

- Sometimes a picture is better than words. Like I mentioned earlier, develop your sketching skills – there are many ways to do this: books, courses etc. Not only will you be better able to communicate with others, but you will communicate better with yourself. If you can graph data, then do so. Think about the best way to visualise the data (quality, project progress, end-user characteristics and anything else that you think needs to be known and shared).

- Sometimes a video is better than a picture – can you use 3D CAD and various types of simulation software?

- Try to make key information as freely available as possible to all others – this is more than putting up a poster or a slide of data. It might require that you change the way information is presented so that everyone can understand and use it. In his book *The Saturn V F-1 Engine*, Anthony Young talks about the briefing program that was used to keep all on the project up to speed with the project and new technologies that were developed. This was a proactive method to ensure shared situational awareness and cognition.

- I will mention this again, but remember that it is not an engineer's responsibility to come up with the best idea. Instead, it is to ensure that the best idea is implemented. Put the effort into properly considering every idea that comes from any part of the team.

If you do ever find that you are the leader of an engineering team, then you can ensure that you have this shared cognition within your team. Do the following:

- Maintain a document of absolute truth. This is a document that is the official record of work that is done. Even if work has actually been done, it is still not officially deemed to have been done until it is recorded as done in this document. The word 'document' is used loosely here. It might be a CAD assembly file where parts are not considered done until they fit properly within the assembly. It might be a live file that records all the design decisions and calculations made. It might also be the accumulated minutes of meetings had by the team. It is important that everyone on the team has access to this document so they can see how the progress of the work is recorded and they can also see what has been done, what needs to be done and how their responsibilities fit in with this progress.

- Ensure you use processes to engage introverts and extraverts. The document of absolute truth is to be a record. If it is only updated in meetings where people need to speak up in front of others, then some team members might not be as forthcoming with information as you would like them to be. Allow for information sharing to occur between smaller groups within the team. You don't need everything to be said in a meeting, but still ensure that everyone has a turn.

- Develop a common language. Does the team talk about how problems have been framed; can they talk about whether they need to coevolve or if someone is fixated? When the team has this common language about engineering practice, they are better able to talk about the progress and needs of an engineering process.

- Encourage people to think systemically. If people are only worried about their own responsibilities, then they might not realise how other people's responsibilities will affect them. You might simply ask that each member acknowledge that they understand each other member's actions to date and the effects of those actions. Maybe at regular intervals each member needs to sign off that they see no issues with the decisions made by other members. There are various ways it can be done, and the best will depend upon the situation. The key goal is to ensure that everyone knows what everyone else is doing.

- Build the team. Teams do not always form naturally. You can get people working as a team by simulating teamwork exercises so that people realise they need to work in teams. However, simply making people understand what others do, how it affects their own work and the project as a whole plays a large role too. When you have this situation, you will have shared situational awareness: everyone understands the challenge faced and the progress in taking on that challenge. All of the previous recommendations ultimately lead toward bringing about this situation. Use that as your measure of how good your team is. Do they all now have the same (and accurate) understanding of the progress of the engineering task they are working on?

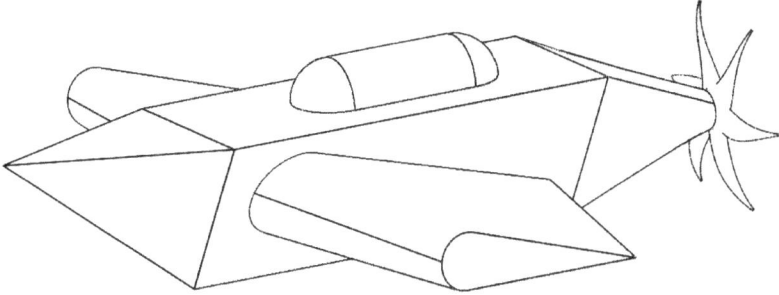

The vehicle designed by a team that did not have shared situational awareness.

4.4 The international team

The previous content of this chapter is applicable for all engineering teams. However, differences in the backgrounds (cultural, economic, organizational and so on) of team members can make implementation more difficult. The following are characteristics of people that can differ with background and can potentially hamper the development of a shared situational awareness.

4.4.1 Communication and writing style

There are a number of writing styles used in different parts of the world that carry over to the general way people communicate. In the west, people often first write what is to be covered, cover the topic and then summarise what has been covered. It is sometimes summarised as:

- Tell 'em what you're going to tell 'em
- Tell 'em
- Tell 'em what you told 'em.

Despite the fact that this seems repetitive, it is intended to make communication fast by drilling the main concept 3 times. To others, such a method of communication can seem to be over so fast that the message is missed. I noticed this in China. As I finished making my point in a meeting, others would be settling in to get the full story, only to be surprised that I (in my opinion) had made my point already.

In a Confucian environment, it is more customary to cover various aspects of the topic being covered and to eventually narrow in on the point that is made. It is described as a spiral approach as the person delivering the message starts talking about the peripheral topics and then gets more specific at the end. I met a technical editor from California, when I was at a tango bar (or milonga) in Tokyo, who had been working for some years in Japan. He confirmed from his experience that academics in Japan did indeed write in such a manner. To a westerner, such writing can seem to lack direction at the start. I have however noticed that people from a confusion culture have very good attention spans and I think that growing up in an environment where information is delivered in such a way helps develop this ability. Team meetings in such a culture can also seem to take longer to reach a conclusion; however, you can be sure that all pertinent topics would have been covered.

The approach often used in Arabic cultures is sometimes called a 'zig-zag' approach. One works towards the conclusion, but the start of each section will summarise the previous section before delivering new information. I was first introduced to this when going through training as an academic to teach multicultural groups. I have also experienced this myself when working with a team of Persians (I use the term 'Arabic' broadly here). In that meeting I noticed how each person, when presenting, would first summarise what the earlier person said and link it to what they were talking about. I was quite impressed – not all the topics were related, I thought, but my colleagues always found a link.

These different styles can cause frustration for people from others backgrounds. Or sometimes they miss key information. Depending upon the situation you will need to either:

- learn to accept knowledge from teammates in a different style,
- learn to deliver information in a different style, or
- encourage a shared style (which might be a mix of the above)

to ensure you are part of a well-functioning team of global engineers.

4.4.2 Specificity of tasks in prior roles

For a team to work well together, members need to have an understanding of what others in the team are doing – shared situational awareness again. However, in economies that are developing, much of the management practice of engineers is more akin to that of managing a factory. This is because of the still developing management pool. Someone who is good at managing a factory could easily find themselves managing an engineering team. Such managers will attempt to break up the engineering tasks and have each engineer focus solely on one task – this is the division of labour that worked so well during, and after, the Industrial Revolution. It works well in factories, but not always in engineering teams.

I conducted research that found engineers who were managed like this found it very difficult to adapt to an integrated team. However, it could be done. If you ever work with an engineer who has come from a company where the engineering tasks have been made very specific, then it will take time for this engineer to change their cognition to be more situationally aware – note the parallels with systemic thinking here. Consider also that maybe you have been working in such an environment, and you might need to work on your ability so that you can improve your situational awareness.

4.4.3 Authority of people over documents (the rule of law)

There is the 'rule of law' and the 'rule of man'. In the former, we obey the written rules (or at least we need to answer to them should we break them). In the second, we do as we are told by the person in charge (or be ready to answer to them). There are no examples of any place in which it is truly a rule of law. However, you will find that the rule of law is less common in developing economies and smaller organisations. In such places, you will find it harder for people to adhere to standard and agreed-upon procedures. This can make it difficult to ensure shared situational awareness; people might complete a task asked of them by an interfering boss (sometimes called 'disrupting the chain of command'), instead of what the plan indicates. It can also limit the success of systems such as Six Sigma; people will not always adhere to the process.

4.4.4 Implied goals

Recall the section on goal analysis. When in a team made of engineers from a background different from yours, you can expect that these engineers will set different inferred goals. This means that you will need to be more explicit when stipulating goals to an international team. It can be expected that others will interpret other goals into what is stated. This usually happens in all engineering teams, but usually everyone in the team is of a similar background; they assume the same implied goals so all goes well. When in an international team, there is a greater diversity of backgrounds. So there is also a greater diversity of goals that can be interpreted into what is presented. Therefore, more information about the project(s) will need to be presented to the team so that everyone knows exactly what is to be delivered.

4.5 Closing on teams

This chapter has been relatively short, but it is important you are aware of the importance of teams within engineering and the need for members to be parts of a whole. Engineering tasks are so complicated these days that you will always need teams. By understanding these nuances of teams, especially international teams, you can be a global engineer.

Using control theory to manage teams - an engineering approach to management

While I have now covered what I wanted to on teams, I want to share this with you in case you too find it useful. Something I found to work with teams, no matter where you are, is the use of a feedback approach instead of feedforward approach in meetings. In most meetings, we say what we need to say and assume others know what we mean and will take congruent action – feedforward. This usually works because of shared backgrounds. When in a mixed team, you are better served using a feedback approach. Once a decision has been made (and you think everyone is on the same page) ask others to respond with what they plan to do next or what outcomes they expect. This helps to reveal what they are thinking. If what they say aligns with other people's understanding of what is to happen, then you can finish the meeting with sufficient confidence that you have achieved shared situational awareness. If it does not, then you now know that you need to adjust and then repeat the message being delivered to the meeting. This will bring everyone to the same state of understanding. Feedback. It could be a meeting between you and another or a meeting of many people. As meetings get larger, you might need to call on only a select number of people (team leaders) or use other methods. One I have tried is putting forward a number of options on what action people think will be taken next and have a show of hands for each option. This was for a team of engineers building a race car – we had about 50 people in the meeting so a lot of potential for different interpretations. You hope everyone will indicate the same option, but they might not. Also, it need not be an actual show of hands. There are anonymous voting applications that you can use. I have found that this approach helps get more participation – especially from introverted types.

5.

Traps and Barriers Against Improvement

Thus far, the focus of this book has been positive. It has talked about what you can do to become better. However, sometimes there are things that you need to avoid. This chapter will focus on things that can hold you back: things that you will want to not do, avoid, or change. Also, much of what I have spoken about earlier has been unique or most common to engineering. The following issues are more generic. They are faced by many professionals, but they are still good for engineers to note.

5.1 Conceptual blocks and creativity

As I mentioned earlier, I am now going to talk more about creativity. However, not about specific and established theories of creativity or how to improve it. There are already numerous books out there that will help you with this. Instead, there are aspects of creativity that are unique to engineering. And a book on how to be an engineer should cover these. Therefore, this section will be focusing specifically upon what aspects of engineering can make creativity difficult. Things known as conceptual blocks.

5.1.1 Is creativity natural?

It has been argued by some I have met in the creativity training space that it is not actually natural for humans to be creative. Children are creative because they can use it to determine how the world works. Once they understand the world they live in (from trial and error of different perspectives) children no longer need this creativity. From this point onwards in their lives, they rely on their established perspective to understand the world.

You can imagine how for the majority of human history (where the environment and way of life were stable) this would be an efficient use of time and mental energy.

However, given that engineers are meant to change the world, a static perspective on the world is not good for us or the people who are having the world changed on them for the better (ideally) by us.

The point that I am making here is that you will need to work at creativity. Because it is important for engineers, but also because there is no evidence that it should come easily. Do not assume that you simply do not have it.

5.1.2 That's the way it's always been done

Many ideas that revolutionise an industry often come from outside that industry. I have seen this happen myself – a really good idea, one that changes a significant aspect of the industry, comes from a customer or an observer of the industry. The reason why this happens is that we get so caught up in the day to day of our jobs that we don't get a chance to step back and really question what we do. It's also natural to automatically do what you did last time – it's easier that way.

However, sometimes, when someone is really struggling with the way things are, they get very creative and come up with new ways of doing things.

I have noticed that salesmen are often a good source of ideas because they are always in contact with the customers who are feeling the pain of working with a less than ideal engineering system. I have also noticed that obnoxious factory workers are good too – they will be more than willing to complain about anything less than optimal. Not two sources you might initially think of as an engineer.

When you're next working on a project and you make a decision, just ask yourself if you're simply doing what's always been done. It might be that you are and that it is indeed the best approach. It's just good to check first.

The hummingbird effect

This is a good place to note the hummingbird effect as described by Steven Johnson in *How we Got to Now*. There are technologies that, once developed, later allow for other technologies. Steven Johnson's book is full of examples. Later on when I talk about the confusion of opinion and fact, be sure to note the anecdote about the development of anti-skid braking systems; it's a similar phenomenon. However, in this instance, the important point to note is that the hummingbird effect refers to the evolution of the hummingbird's wings only after the coevolution of flowers (and nectar) with pollen carrying insects; and how this can be an analogy for technology. There are two things to note from the hummingbird effect as a global engineer:

1. It might be time now to change how things are done due to other changes in technology or society (think about how

the development of mobile phones affected the market for cameras). Consider such things each time a new idea is presented.

2. When you are in a different part of the world with different ubiquitous technologies, economics and social makeup, realise that what worked in one place might not work in another. Also think about why things are done the way they are being done. Think about how a society/culture that is stricter with roles would not produce tradespeople who will take as much initiative in development – I noticed this going from the west to China where I needed to be clearer with designs/ideas or clearer that I would value a tradesperson's input.

5.1.3 Not invented here

This can be confused with the previous block. You might simply assume that people with new ideas do not understand why things are the way they are. However, this dismissal of a new idea from outside your organization is often because of identity. Many engineers think that, as the engineer, they are meant to be the one who comes up with the ideas. I also recall engineers, when I was in the automotive industry, calling this phenomenon the "I invented it syndrome". Where people wanted to push their own ideas (recall the discussion on attachment as a form of fixation in chapter 2). However, an idea can come from anywhere, and as an engineer, you need a shift in attitude to ensure the best ideas are used.

It is not the engineer's role to come up with the best idea; it is the engineer's role to see that the best idea is used.

I am not suggesting that you should give up on being creative. You should do your utmost to be creative. Just don't let this desire stop you from adopting the good ideas of others or developing upon them. If you can get as many ideas as you can out of those around you, then whatever it is that you're engineering will be better.

Also remember that you will always be the engineer so giving credit to others for coming up with a good idea will do no harm to your reputation and people will appreciate your praise. Then these people will share more ideas with you. With these ideas, you will be able to engineer even better systems. I have seen this happen numerous times, and know it works.

There is an even greater hazard associated with this conceptual block: when it becomes part of a culture in a company. Your entire company will suffer when this happens, but you will likely not even notice it. Around the world there are many research organizations. Often, they are governmental, and their role is to simply generate knowledge for others to use – think of universities as one example. If companies do not actively employ their engineers to better understand this freely available (and often rigorous) knowledge, then these companies will never be able to benefit from this knowledge. Think about all those lost opportunities and substandard engineering, simply because people do not like ideas from outside.

If you get the chance, read *Hitting the Brakes* by Ann Johnson. It provides many insights into how technologies are developed (using the development of anti-lock braking systems as a case study). It also gives an interesting example where a British research laboratory generated considerable amounts of useful information, but British industry still failed to progress from the knowledge. However, at the same time companies in Germany, France and Sweden readily subscribed to publications by the laboratory. For some reason, British companies did not choose to put the effort into taking advantage of this clearly beneficial knowledge. If you ever become an engineering manager, try to ensure your company doesn't fail to benefit from useful knowledge that has come from outside your organization.

Obviously, dismissing outsider knowledge runs counter to being a global engineer. However, I have seen this taken to even greater extremes. Where a new engineer is sure that everything (knowledge, procedures, and attitude) they have brought with them is better than what is within their new company. Based on my personal experience and the research I have conducted into this topic while in academia, this seems most common when engineers relocate from Europe or North America to other parts of the world. It even happens when engineers relocate from Europe to North America, or vice versa or even within either of the respective continents. Just so you know – I have rarely seen a case where the engineer in question actually did have anything better to offer. People often assume that if they come from a country (or region or company) with a longer and richer history in engineering (and some places certainly do have this), then they, as an individual, must be special in some way. Take a look at the sections on background in chapter 6 to get a better understanding of why people are sometimes so sure that they bring something better – and try to not be like that.

5.1.4 Artificial constraints

It is quite normal for people to make associations with things and let those associations constrain the ideas they generate. This is sometimes called 'functional fixedness'. People might also talk about not thinking outside the box. Essentially, we make assumptions about things and assume that they need to be used that way. The most common example that I have come across is the barometer example.

Question: How do you use a barometer to determine the height of a building?

Functional fixedness answer 1: A barometer measures pressure so we can measure the pressure at the top and bottom of the building and use the formula for the pressure of a fluid under gravity to work out the height.

Functional fixedness answer 2: A barometer is heavy so we can attach a rope to it and lower the barometer from the top of the building while measuring the rope used. When the tension reduces, the barometer has touched the ground. The length of rope measured is the height of the building.

Functional fixedness answer 3: A barometer is subject to the laws of gravity. If we drop it over the edge of the building and measure the time it took to fall, then we can determine the height it fell, and thus the height of the building.

The above shows how we can be constrained artificially by our own ideas about how things can work. If you haven't seen it, then also look up the various solutions to drawing through all the dots in a 3x3 array with 4 or fewer lines – the solutions you will see are more examples of how you can expand your perception to allow for more possible solutions.

An important reason why I covered this issue is that, as engineers, we frequently use numerous tools for specific tasks. Often, we are proud of the knowledge we have about these tools and their intended use. Thus, we can tend to view many things as having a set use or purpose. We are perhaps more likely than others to suffer from artificial constraints.

If you think you might have this tendency – and you probably do (we all do) – then, every once in a while, think about a random device and how you could use it to help solve a problem that you're working on. It will help reduce this tendency and possibly bring in some new ideas. Don't worry – if it turns out not to help, then you do not need to tell people what you were thinking.

5.1.5 Assumed conditions

This one actually gets me a bit – I often assume that something is a fixed condition beyond questioning. This is similar to, but different from, artificial constraints. Instead of us imposing a constraint we take a challenge at face value and assume the implicit conditions. We then think about how we can operate within those conditions. The anecdote I mentioned earlier in chapter 2 about sealing with an O-ring is an example of assumed conditions. People thought theory had let them down, but they had incorrectly assumed that the sealing surface was smooth when it was not.

The solution to this block is to ask as many questions as you can about the respective situation. Put the effort into asking more questions, and you will dig deeper. Hopefully, you will ask a question like: how rough is that surface? Then those assumed conditions that limit your view of the situation, and your creativity, will be gone.

5.1.6 Thinking an idea is a solution

You're likely familiar with the quote of Thomas Edison 'Genius is one percent inspiration and ninety-nine percent perspiration.' This is true of creativity in engineering too. We sometimes feel that once we get the idea, we're done. We relax. However, putting a creative idea into action is a lot of work. Getting the idea is just the beginning. Don't pat yourself on the back until the solution is actually working. This will help prevent you from fixating – or suffering from the 'I invented it syndrome'. If you focus on the solution alone, then you will be more open to other ideas if the one you're pursuing is proving unviable.

5.1.7 Thinking creativity is a mysterious thing that must be spontaneous

Certainly, we can all recall times when we just had an idea come from nothing – it seemed to be like magic. We can be forgiven for thinking that creativity is a unique talent beyond our control when we experience this. However, there are other approaches that can be used to develop good ideas. These might or might not be the same as creativity, but the effect is pretty similar. Thus, do not shy away from the numerous methods out there to help people be creative. The classic for Engineers is TRIZ and derivatives of methods like this. A German colleague of mine said he started coming up with numerous ideas that were of higher quality once he started using such methods. I have found De Bono's Six Hats ideal as well. The key to these tools is that they make you look at a problem in a certain way that allows you to conceive new ideas. If you are ever having troubles being creative, then do not shy away from using some formal and systematic tools to help.

5.2 The way you choose to think

Many think that the way they think is beyond their control and it just happens. However, you are capable of meta-cognition: thinking about how to think. By being aware of how you tend to think or how you are thinking about a specific problem (causing issues solving that problem), you then are able to consider how else to think so that you can better tackle that same problem (or any other problem).

Thinking about the way you choose to think will be the focus here.

5.2.1 Not managing your sensing tendencies – no time to be passive

We each have preferred ways to perceive the world. Sometimes, these preferred tendencies are exactly what are needed. At other times they are not. By understanding your tendencies and thinking about which ones are most suitable for a given task, you can better determine and better perceive any problem.

You can then conceive an ideal solution. The three major ways we perceive the world are VAK:

- Visual
- Auditory
- Kinaesthetic

If you have a visual tendency, then you will like graphs to display information, you will say things like 'I see what you mean', you will notice what people wear more than what they say – perhaps not pick up tones in their voice, and misunderstand subtle messages, and possibly doodle a lot.

If you have an auditory tendency, then you will like closing your eyes and listening to music more so than others, you will say things like 'I hear what you mean', you will listen to people's words and perhaps not notice the expression on their face or their posture.

If you're a kinaesthetic person, then you will usually need to do something to understand it (someone telling you about it or seeing it is not enough), you will say things like 'I feel that this is a good idea', you will pick up on people's mood more than notice what they say or how they look, and appreciate the feel of clothes more than the looks.

If you want to know your preference, then there are many online surveys that you can take. Type the words 'VAK', 'modality' and 'survey' into any search engine, and you will find a free one that you can take to find your preferences. Chances are you have a good idea already.

Typically, engineers are most likely to be visual, then next likely to be kinaesthetic and least likely to be auditory. Considering that most engineering degrees are taught using lectures, which favour the auditory, we are lucky to have any engineers at all. We have probably also lost some potentially excellent engineers: those who could not handle the auditory approach used to teach engineering, and then dropped out.

An anecdote – how modalities can work against us

In a period of my life when I was an academic, I had a student who showed phenomenal promise of being a great engineer, but who rarely performed well academically. How did I know he would most likely be a good engineer? I had the chance to see him as a member of the Formula-SAE team (where students design, build and race an open wheeled racer). As part of this team, this student showed an ability to get the job done, fix problems as they presented, and craft clever solutions. Once the problem was real, he was in his element. At other times he found the going hard. He once told me that he felt frustrated watching TV – to demonstrate how trying he found lectures. You might have realised by now that he had very strong kinaesthetic tendencies. Telling him what to do or even showing him how to do something was simply not enough. He needed to be doing something to make it real enough for him. Otherwise, it was just abstract and a waste of time.

This anecdote was to show how your tendencies can make something hard. If you do not realise that it's just a tendency, then you might think that you just can't do something. It might be more of a challenge to change your sensing, as I said to this student, but once you know the real issue, you can start doing something about it.

As we get older, we tend to balance out our tendencies and we can use the modality that is required for each problem we encounter. It's simply too hard to get by in this world with only one modality. However, we can still have different tendencies in different situations and not knowing the best one for a given tendency could mean that we're not getting a full understanding of things. If this happens, then we're not being the best engineer we can be.

So what's the best sensing tendency for an engineer to have?

If only it were that simple. The fact is that at times you will need to *visualise* a solution, and at other times you will need to **physically** put the solution into place or experience the problem **firsthand**. Sometimes you will need to *listen* to the user of a system before you can *feel* their frustration with a current system. And then you will need to *look* deeply into a system before you can really understand what's going on.

I have made the words associated with sensing bold and italic to show how as an engineer you will need to use a variety of senses to understand problems and develop solutions. Thus, as an engineer, you will need to develop all of your senses. As I said above, we naturally become more balanced in our sensing tendencies with age, but don't be passive about this. Put the effort into using all your senses.

When you do use all your senses, you will be surprised at how much of the world – including your engineering world – was unknown to you. But once this is known, you will understand problems better and thus implement much better engineering solutions.

It is worth noting that others have argued strongly for visualization being the most important thing for engineering. Eugene S. Ferguson's *Engineering and the Mind's Eye* is an excellent example of this. However, even in this work, the other senses and their importance in developing engineering ability are noted. I can recall my father showing me a loose wheel bearing on a car. Feeling it by hand made me think it was fine – the movement was minor. However, when the car was moving at speed, this small movement had a major effect on the steering and handling. Years later, I encountered another bearing problem where what felt like a small bump in the inner or outer race (as the balls went over it), caused a huge noise when in operation. Various experiences like these, where one can link the feel of something with the visuals of a car not steering well or a machine making loud noise, allow an engineer to develop a much better understanding of how engineering systems actually work.

Your development as an engineer must be sensual (using all senses). This is also the characteristic of a good engineering education. Around the world there are different approaches to engineering education. Some will lean towards auditory methods and some will have more opportunity to be kinaesthetic. Therefore, you will likely have been encouraged to develop a certain sensing profile. Just as others will have developed another profile. When you work with engineers from other places (possibly in the same country, but from a different educational institution) you will need to be prepared to work with people who sense differently. As a guide, an auditory approach to education is the cheapest and kinaesthetic the most expensive. Thus, the less an educator invests in the education of its engineering students, the more likely they are to be auditory.

Sensing and intuition

I mention intuition a few times in this book. Now is an ideal time to expand upon this topic. Have you noticed that you know what intuition is, but you can't quite describe it and you don't know where it comes from? Intuition comes from a broad contemplation of something: logically, emotionally, physically, conceptually and so on. You contemplate something from so many perspectives that you can no longer hold a single thought about it in your head. Further, you do this in a context where you can contemplate this something often and get instant feedback on how it behaves (as mentioned by Daniel Kahneman in his book *Thinking, Fast and Slow*). You then seem to be guided by a general sense of what to do. When you work on broadening your sensing tendencies, you will enter this intuitive state. Many cultures around the world will limit the physical aspects of their education of professionals, some more than others, assuming professionals are not meant to work with their hands, and thus culture could limit your ability to develop your full engineering intuition.

5.2.2 Procedural thinking

One of the tendencies often developed in an engineering degree is procedural thinking. This comes from the large amount of scientific knowledge that an engineer needs to prove an understanding of before graduating. Much of this knowledge is evaluated by applying related procedures to demonstrate an ability to use theory to solve for unknowns. For example, the temperature on either side of a wall subject to a thermal energy transfer, the deflection of a beam subject to a force and the voltage drop across a circuit.

Think about the number of exams that you have to complete to pass an engineering degree and the amount of study for each, all of which would often involve following a procedure of some sort again and again. It is easy to see how this could at least promote procedural thinking. However, the worst thing it can do is leave some engineers only able to think in such a way.

Procedural thinking can get you through an engineering degree, but it will be a huge liability as an engineer when you need to take on problems with no clear solution. In these cases, dealing with ill-defined problems, you will need to consider your options (maybe even create one), choose one, try it, and then maybe try another if the first one doesn't work. If you're accustomed to thinking procedurally, then this can be very confronting, and be a hit to your confidence.

Throughout this book, I have spoken about various types of thinking that are the opposite to procedural thinking. Framing, systemic thinking and first principles require you to understand the situation, identify the appropriate theory yourself and then formulate the problem that you will choose to solve. Working on these abilities will encourage a more flexible type of thinking, and help you move away from excessive procedural thinking. However, simply engaging in the meta-cognition I have spoken about earlier, where you think about your thinking process, will serve you well.

For now though, ask yourself the following questions:

- How much did I rely on my ability to recall formulae and procedures to get through my engineering degree?
- How well do I really think I understood the theory that I was meant to learn?
- When I come across an engineering problem, do I have trouble moving forward if I:
  - can't recall exactly what to do, or
  - feel I don't have all the information needed?
- Do I ever wish engineering problems were presented to me in a certain way so that it is easier for me to work out what needs to be done or so that my role is clearer?

If answering these questions makes you think that you have a tendency for procedural thinking, then you know you likely need to work on being less procedural (and more adaptable).

It should be pointed out that procedural thinking is not bad. There are many times when a set procedure is exactly what's needed. You might ask yourself if you are actually hostile to procedures. There's certainly no point in trying to derive a new way of designing something if there is already a standard that lays everything out for you. Standards, which I will talk about later, and the procedures within them, were written by experts on the topic. They probably know a lot more about the topic than you do so any deviation on your part is likely to lead to something sub-optimal.

The irony is that some people who are focused on procedures are unable to work out which procedure to use, and even need a procedure to choose the right procedure. Thus, you need to develop an ability to consider the role of procedural think on a case-by-case basis. This can even be each time you shift from coming up with a solution, to documenting the solution, and then to implementing the solution. As the benefits and limitations of procedural over non-procedural thinking change from stage to stage.

5.2.3 Not taking your time when you need to

This is possibly more applicable to engineering managers, but all engineers need to be aware of it. Sometimes it takes a while to understand what the real issue is. Recall framing and coevolution from earlier. However, some of us want to see action straight away. I have noticed personally that this can be a result of background. In an environment where there are not the economic resources desired, it might not seem possible to let an engineer take their time to really come to terms with a problem so that they can come up with an optimal solution. If you are confronting a serious problem, then you will probably need to expect that a lot of time and work will be required — especially when it comes to understanding the problem and developing a strategy for solving this problem. This can cause frustration for managers and other observers, but such work is essential. An engineer can also feel pressure from others to look like they are working instead of actually working (even though it sometimes does not look it).

Anecdote – understanding versus doing

Some years before writing this, I had a colleague who was part of a research project that involved a number of companies, universities and government. The goal was to develop an array of technologies that would help progress the local drive-by-wire industry. My colleague was in a company that was new to the research game. This meant his manager didn't understand some of the aspects of good engineering research. One of them being first understanding existing theory so that the research efforts can be efficiently and precisely applied. My colleague was effectively chastised each time he was 'caught' reading and received nods of approval when he was building prototypes. The manager had little appreciation of how much time should be spent understanding the problem, and thus preferred a random search approach. The company in question is no longer in business.

Some engineers will also feel frustration when applying first principles. When this happens, you might feel that you are not making sufficient progress. Always try to be objective about how long it should take to apply first principles and how much time would be saved by not spending it on a random search.

If Edison had a needle to find in a haystack, he would proceed at once with the diligence of the bee to examine straw after straw until he found the object of his search. I was a sorry witness of such doings, knowing that a little theory and calculation would have saved him ninety per cent of his labor . — Nikola Tesla (from TESLA SAYS EDISON WAS AN EMPIRICIST New York Times October 19th, 1931)

Formulating your ideas can seem unproductive to others, and maybe even to you, but give this essential formulation time; you will make fewer costly mistakes later.

5.2.4 Logic – or a lack thereof

Have you ever come across people who act like they know what is going on even though they don't? They can actually seem very confident, while you, on the other hand, seem less certain; even though you know that you know more.

Hopefully you have. Otherwise, you're possibly one of those people. Someone who is not competent, but thinks that they are. The phenomenon is called the Dunning–Kruger effect, named after two researchers who studied this phenomenon in the late 1990s.

It is an interesting phenomenon: as we know more, we become less certain. We can see how complex things are. This can make us not commit – 'paralysis by analysis' as some have called it. Ignorant people, on the other hand, with no ability to see how complex something is, can happily progress forward in their ignorance.

This can cause all sorts of problems when ignorant people start doing things. However, I find it most annoying when these people meet with success.

The reason that ignorant people succeed at times is that they at least made a decision (note the section on Indecisiveness) and they were probably lucky (which, as yet, can't be developed).

This produces a paradox. As we become more knowledgeable, we become less certain, which can mean that others seem more confident. Because engineering is very much about gaining more knowledge, it is likely that many engineers will become less certain and less able to convince others – simply because more knowledge makes them less certain. Therefore, engineers need to know how to be sure they are right when they actually are. Which does seem like a strange thing to need.

It would also be good to know how to ensure when we are confident that we are not simply ignorant. And it would be good to be able to find holes in the proposed plans of others, and not be swayed by their ignorance augmented confidence.

The solution to all these issues is logic.

If you can create a logical argument for your contention, you are relying on something more than an inability to see alternatives. Furthermore, you can break others' ideas down into a series of logical arguments to see if they actually stack up to the scrutiny.

The logic itself should not be difficult; much of engineering is inherently logical. However, engineers are rarely taught a disciplined way to express logic within an argument, or to analyse logic.

There are numerous ways to study logic, and if you're really keen, then a course in critical thinking is ideal.

However, the Toulmin Analysis of an Argument, developed by Stephen Toulmin, is, in my experience, the best way to help engineers understand the expression of logic. In this analysis there are three basic elements of an argument:

1. The claim. This is basically the point you wish to make. For example, you might be making the point that aluminium should be used in a design despite the fact that it will eventually fatigue.

2. The grounds. This is information that is known. It's basically the facts at hand. For example, the facts might be that the designed system will be used in salt water, which corrodes steel at a much faster rate than the steel will fatigue under the estimated cyclic loading.

3. The warrant. This is what links the grounds to the claim. In the example that I am using, you can probably already see

it; sometimes the warrant is obvious. However, this is the logical part, and you might need to be explicit to ensure that everyone understands. For example, you might show the life of steel in salt water and the life of aluminium under the cyclic loading, then note that the life of the aluminium is greater. The greater life makes for a better product, and the claim that aluminium should be used is hard to disagree with.

Someone else might come back with a counterargument that it is easy enough to use a sacrificial anode, and using this with a steel design is better again. However, they have at least been logical, and you know what their logic is.

Note how logic complements decision making and separating fact from opinion.

Next time you need to make a point or convince others of something using your engineering knowledge, first identify the claim, grounds and warrant of your point. Then convert those into a cogent argument to be presented to others.

5.2.5 Not knowing what you don't know

It can seem that there is something of an oxymoron within this heading. If you know what you don't know, then you know it. Thus, it is known, and not unknown. However, this is not quite what I mean. I am talking about understanding the limitations on your knowledge. Then either accepting that this represents uncertainty you need to work with – see the section uncertainty that is coming – or, in this instance, knowing that gap in your knowledge should be filled by another. This is opposed to assuming that you need to rely on your knowledge alone.

I have mentioned concurrent engineering a few times in this book. If you practice this, and work well in a team, then you will naturally fill these gaps. However, as I will show in the anecdote below, we sometimes forget to consider what we don't know, and make overly compromised decisions.

Anecdote – what tradespeople know and you probably don't

This is an example from early in my career and still comes to my mind on a regular basis. At the time, I was working for a company that designed and made unique mining equipment. One of my colleagues had been working on a design for some period. He wanted to ensure that everything he designed could be easily made and assembled. Therefore, no part was deemed finished until he was sure it could be made with sufficient ease. When the drawings were handed to the supplier (who was a qualified tradesperson and also liked to show an interest in what we made), he asked why the parts had been designed as they were and suggested a better way to design them. The suggestions were the same as my colleague's initial ideas that were dismissed because he concluded that they were too difficult to manufacture. The supplier then explained how they could be made. These were sufficiently easy operations, but they were unknown to my colleague. If the company did not have a supplier that was as interested as this one was, then the final system would have been unnecessarily compromised and not much cheaper to produce. By not realising that he was not expert in manufacture, my colleague was limiting the potential of his work. Simply engaging with the supplier as part of the team early on, congruent with concurrent engineering, would have resolved this issue.

The above anecdote shows the value in working with others. However, it can also make those engineers who were a tradesperson before being an engineer assume they have this covered. This too can be dangerous. Recall the case I mentioned earlier about the panel beater who used his skills to fix a door when there was a better way – he was unaware of what other trades people would know. I also recall my father – who was a fitter and turner (before the term machinist become the norm) – noting how much boiler makers knew that he did not. As helpful as a trade can be one still needs to accept that many others know what one does not know. This also ignores the progression that can occur within a trade (progression that you are likely unaware of once you leave that trade). Knowledge can become dated faster than we often realise. In short, it is wise to check with others who are expert in the respective field so that you know what you don't know. Because you don't know what you don't know until somebody tells you so.

5.2.6 A lack of morals

This might seem odd, but this issue is related to standards. Research into where engineers think their responsibility ends has shown that they often rely upon standards to determine if an item they are developing is safe. This is opposed to their judgment as professional engineers. In short, the law or regulation is used as a proxy for ethics. We assume that these are sufficiently well thought out, and can be used to remove the need for moral responsibility and focusing on the improvement of society. However, these standards can vary from place to place. Thus, the quality that you offer to those utilising anything you work on will also vary if you rely on standards alone. Consider the broader implications of your decisions within the context of both standards and your location to ensure your engineering standard is not hindered when you work in another part of the world.

As a practising engineer, I am aware that many others will argue for engineers to be ethical without acknowledging the other factors that influence engineering decision making. Factors such as the ethics of the employer and society in general. Thus, you should use morals as much as you can. If you feel that the morals of your employer or the element of society that utilises what you work on are significantly different from your own, then it is up to you as an individual to decide if a career change is needed.

What I am essentially arguing here is that you need to consider morals to make yourself more universal as standards change from one part of the world to the other.

5.3 You!

Sometimes it is you. There are just things about you that can hold you back from being a better engineer and one that can be successful anywhere in the world. These can be the hardest to confront. We are all happy with who we are. If we were not, then we would be changing naturally. You therefore need to consider yourself objectively and think about what can be changed so that you are a global engineer.

5.3.1 Being unprepared to change and responsibility

In section 5.2, I mentioned a number of influences upon the type of engineer that you are or will become. There have already been years of influence upon you. Without needing to take any action you have been made into what you are.

That means, you will likely need to take action and turn yourself into what you want to be. But, even if you overcome the fear of change, you might simply find that these changes are hard work. You need to focus on changing yourself and, sometimes, push yourself to do it. You might also think that you shouldn't need to change yourself.

It can be a bit like the notion of identity, you will use the excuse of being true to yourself to justify not changing.

What's important is that you take full responsibility for yourself and who you are. By doing this, you are ready to be who you want to be.

Now, if you like who you are, then that's good. It's quite likely that if I met you then I would like you too. I like people who are interested in understanding what they can do to be better at something and the fact that you're reading this book means that you are one of these people. This, however, doesn't mean that you can't change. Remember the following:

> Improvement is a type of change; if you're not prepared to change, then you can't improve.

This statement is true of everything in life. As we grow, we need to change and adapt. Do not shy away from this. Instead, take responsibility for yourself and the type of person you want to be. The truth is that once your parents have raised you, you are responsible for who you are and who you become. It is not true that you have no control over this. And it is not true that you will always be who you are now. Take control, and use what you have learnt in this book to become a better engineer.

There is a lot of research and advice on how to change yourself. Reproducing this knowledge here is beyond the scope of this book. However, one key to successful change is your perception of the future. Are you the type of person who can happily work on something because you can see the benefits it will bring in the future or are you the type of person who would rather just live in the moment? Chances are that you have a fairly strong future focus; you wouldn't take on engineering otherwise. However, we all have a tendency to live in the moment. I know that I do. As you read through the techniques within this book on how to be a better engineer, imagine having those abilities in the future and imagine them getting better. Not only that, but imagine them getting better as a result of you putting the effort into applying these techniques. This will help you maintain that focus to change and improve yourself.

5.3.2 Confidence and identity

Sometimes, it can be a shock to learn that we still have room to improve. Sometimes, we can be fearful of becoming good at something that we have never really worked on before.

This can be very true of applying first principles. Systemic thinking can be worked on easily because it often comes with experience. Framing is the sort of thing that has a number of possible answers, even though there are more wrong answers. When you come up with another frame you have essentially come up with another idea – which is hard to argue is right or wrong - so there is less fear of failure. However, first principles are typically either right or wrong, and a mistake is very clear. Also, we sometimes feel apprehensive if we can't instantly determine which principles we should be applying. This clarity in mistake identification, and the resulting apprehension, can make the application of first principles something to be feared.

This fear can then make us resort to excuses for not using first principles. We might say we can't be expected to because of our background (experience, education, study approach, time since we graduated, what's worked for us in the past and so on). We basically use our identity to justify not changing.

However, your identity within this context is that you are an engineer.

Ask yourself this question: If you, as the engineer, are not the one who will use first principles (or any other attribute) to analyse and optimise a solution to a problem, then who will? I can't think of anyone other than an engineer who would do this. That means if someone else does it, then they are a better engineer, and that's who you want to be. Therefore, you need to confront any fears you might have about taking on the challenge of becoming a better engineer.

To become one, you will need to confront the fear of failing to possess the attributes of a global engineer.

Confronting fears is very much an issue of emotional maturity. This might not seem like something that engineers are renowned for (all this touchy-feely liberal arts stuff that we hoped to avoid by choosing engineering to study). However, this is a case where you need it. You need to manage your feelings. If you start to feel overwhelmed with a problem that seems too complex, or you worry you can't work out the theory that is applicable for a particular problem, or if you are frustrated because you just can't see behind the problem to the real engineering problem, then it is time to take control of your emotions. The term observing ego has been used to describe this. Observe yourself. Be aware of how you are feeling. Decide how you think you should feel. Then work toward inducing this feeling. Some of us are better at this than others, but remaining sufficiently calm and relaxed, while still keeping your motivation, so that your mind works at its best, should always be your goal. When you can do this, you will not only be a competent engineer, but you will also remain cool under pressure. This is an excellent ability to have.

Something to ponder

It was argued in *Hitting the Brakes* by Ann Johnson that it took quite some time for electronic controls and related technology to become established in the automotive industry. It has also been suggested by some that if there were more electrical engineers in the automotive industry, then we would have had functional electric cars decades ago. Could it be that the majority of mechanical engineers in the auto industry were not willing to understand electronics or electric motor technology, and they slowed the introduction of this technology? If so, then is it possible that at times you have been dismissive of an idea or technology simply because you did not understand it and felt that it was beyond you to do so? What will you try to do next time a new technology, one that potentially devalues your current expertise, is presented to you? Try to dismiss it or learn about it and master it?

The engineering stereotype and the real driver of technology

Something that you notice when you work in different parts of the world is that there is a stereotype about the type of person who becomes an engineer. In many places, the typical engineer is male. This can help to explain why in many parts of the world, there is still an underrepresentation of women in engineering - a self fulfilling prophecy. However, I studied with an engineer whose father was Ukrainian, and was not surprised when his daughter chose mechanical engineering. Many mechanical engineers in the Ukraine were female when compared to Australia.

The other stereotype can be ethnic. Azealia Banks (you might not know her because she is a rapper so not someone you expect to be cited in a book on engineering) noted that many people of an African background in a predominantly white society will assume they aren't the stereotypical engineer (in an interview on Hot 97 - Dec 19, 2014). This is because, in many places, the history of technology focuses on inventors that most people can associate with. Many technologies are developed simultaneously in different parts of the world. However, we do usually focus on the inventor closer to us. You probably know of the dual invention of calculus by Leibnitz and Newton. However, others had contributed to this earlier. A few Greek friends of mine maintain that it was Archimedes who really invented calculus. You can often argue that your favoured person was the inventor by 'massaging' the definition of invention. By doing this we can then create the stereotype of what an inventor is - and by default a stereotypical engineer who invents technology.

However, there is another perspective we can take on engineering - one that removes our identity as a factor in what makes an engineer.

Recall the hummingbird effect mentioned earlier? It was from the book *How we Got to Now* by Steven Johnson. In this book, Steven Johnson looks at the evolution of key technologies and inventions from the perspective of machines. In this perspective, humans are the tools that evolve technology, and the evolution of technology is more a function of earlier technologies. With this perspective, you can see how it is that common inventions present in multiple separate places at the same time (or around the same time). Technological progression is less about us and more about the opportunities and drivers presented by prior technology and current needs. When we focus more on technology as something that develops as long as it is given attention, and stop thinking that it is something unique in the inventor (which seems to be a natural tendency that we have), then we realise that anyone can be an engineer. And that as long as we develop the needed skills, we can be both excellent and global engineers.

5.3.3 Willpower

Willpower is interesting for two reasons. Firstly, willpower is likely to be essential so you can continually monitor your thinking as you improve it, or for when you're solving some of the more challenging engineering problems. Secondly, research into willpower has shown that it is indeed a type of power, which engineers understand well. If you're low on energy, then you will lack willpower. And as an engineer, you will need willpower.

Willpower in everyday engineering

Two of the best engineers I ever worked with were great engineers because they would never leave a problem until they knew that they had cracked it. It might have been a design where they wanted to ensure that every dimension was set for a reason. It might have been finding the cause of a failure and ruling out all other possible causes to ensure that the true cause was known. Regardless of the situation, they never fatigued and kept on working on the problem at hand until it was resolved. This is the kind of willpower all engineers need. It's the only way you can ensure that a problem is properly solved. In *The Unwritten Laws of Engineering*, W.J. King calls this 'tenacity' and covers it on the second page of his book when talking about the need to show an ability to get things done.

Willpower to become a better engineer

Much of what has been covered in this book will require change on your part if you are to take advantage of it. And it's a very challenging type of change too. You need to continually monitor your thinking. This can be taxing, and if you do not have the willpower to keep monitoring it, then you will regress to your old habits.

Building willpower

As I said above, willpower has been found to indeed be a form of power. That means you need to fuel it and be careful about what you're focusing it on. If you're in the process of improving your engineering by monitoring your thinking, or if you're working on a challenging project as an engineer, then remember the following:

- It will be harder to do if you're also working on something else, like quitting smoking or dieting for example, which demands willpower. It is best to choose one or the other, but not both. Otherwise, you're setting yourself up to fail. Unless, all of these actions are part of the one goal of overall improvement, and they support each other in your mind. In such cases, failing at one makes it easier to fail at the others.

- You need energy. Don't take on challenging problems or try to monitor your thinking while you're hungry. Once again, you're setting yourself up to fail.

- Don't let work be a case of willpower. If you're continually working against people who are not trying to work in a manner congruent with being a better engineer, then it will be that much harder; it will sap the willpower you need for your job and self-improvement. If you think another company might have a culture congruent with better engineering practice, then give serious thought to changing jobs. Otherwise, try to work in a way where others are not making it harder for you to improve the way you work.

- You will not always need willpower. Once your new way of working as an engineer becomes habit – where thinking about your thinking becomes natural so that it's always improving – you will no longer need willpower for it. You can then try to quit smoking or going on that diet (or maybe that's done before investing in your engineering ability).

The important thing to note here is that changing to become a better engineer will not always be easy, and that as an engineer, you sometimes need to dig deep – it can be that the better engineer is simply the one who stuck at the problem for longer. But if you are interested in learning more about this, then Roy Baumeister and John Tierney's *Willpower: Why Self-Control is the Secret to*

Success is an excellent source of information for anyone wanting to improve their willpower.

5.3.4 Discomfort with uncertainty

In much of this book, I have encouraged you to use first principles to find optimum and exact answers. I have also spoken about framing, so that you define the problem, and systemic thinking, so that all your decisions will have only known (and acceptable) consequences. This is, in some respects, counter to things such as coevolution. The fact is that there will always be some uncertainty. You need to minimise it, but you still need to live with it.

Think now where you are on the spectrum between being happy to take on a task without knowing what might happen, through to needing so much certainty that you rarely take action.

Ideally, you want to be a person who can take on things on a case-by-case basis. You need to consider what uncertainty can be eliminated with ease and what will take so much time to resolve that you might as well start working on the task at hand – and resolve the uncertainty as you do. I wish I could give you more guidance on this, but by its nature this is hard to prescribe. Nevertheless, simply considering the effort to resolve the uncertainty in comparison to the related task at hand is a very good start.

5.3.5 Desire for sophistication

Sometimes we assume that things need to be sophisticated and complicated to be good. This is a bit like goal analysis (2.2.1), but unique to engineers. As an engineer you will sometimes feel that if a solution doesn't seem sufficiently complex, then you have not done your job as an engineer. Logically, I am sure you know that there is nothing ingenious about making something more complex than it needs to be. However, you can still feel that a simple solution or one that was easy to implement was not a proper use of your skills. There is nothing wrong with implementing a standard established solution, or one that was developed by someone who is not an engineer. Like creativity, as an engineer, you simply want to ensure that the best idea is implemented; not that it is your idea that is implemented.

I have witnessed potentially good ideas ruined by engineers wanting to add extra features. Features that were impressive in their own right, but for the customer simply added cost. In fact, I know of a case where this desire on the part of engineers increased the cost of a system to double what the customer was willing to pay. What was even more concerning was that these engineers were actually reconfiguring working pieces of machinery to feel they had contributed something substantial to the final product and ignored excellent simplifying suggestions from others – probably because the others were tradesmen and because the engineers wanted to ensure they could 'feel like' (as opposed to 'know') they were being engineers.

Always focus on what needs to be done. And be sure you evaluate the suitability of a solution in an informed and logical way that is free of ego or desire to prove yourself as an engineer. This means framing properly and being aware of the way you analyse your goals.

Note that I am not advocating simplicity for its own sake here – although simple systems are usually cheaper, more reliable and of greater quality. Just that you should focus on solving the problem as opposed to being impressed by complexity or sophistication.

5.3.6 Indecisiveness

This is often a lesson that is to be learned by young engineers. Engineers will sometimes see a number of options that can be taken when confronting a problem. This is usually good. As I have said earlier, having a lot of ideas is a good way to have a good idea. However, you do eventually need to choose one to develop further. And this is not as easy as it sounds.

Making a decision can in fact take willpower. You can see advantages to each of your ideas, but by choosing one you then think about the advantages of all the other ideas that you're losing by not developing those other ideas. This is the source of indecision.

Indecisiveness seems to be a natural tendency. One we need to grow out of. And once upon a time we would have. If you were in a drought-stricken area and you had a choice of going either East or West, then you would know that you need to make that decision pretty quickly; because you know that you would die otherwise. We rarely confront such situations today (especially if you grew up in a wealthy western country – where people are less decisive). Thus, we have had little opportunity to exercise our ability to let go of many ideas (and all their innate advantages and opportunities) to pursue just one. It is being able to let go of these other ideas that can require willpower.

I have seen engineers afflicted with this problem numerous times. Don't be one of them. Try this.

> **First**, accept the fact that you need to let most ideas go.
>
> **Second**, think of ways to rank ideas – this is where experience can help a lot, but understanding the real problem (framing) and analysing it (first principles) and thinking about the implications of an idea (systemic thinking) can help work out criteria.
>
> **Third**, use the ranking to find the best idea.
>
> **Fourth**, choose an idea (likely the topped rank one) and develop it.
>
> **Fifth**, don't look back unless you are sure that you have chosen the wrong idea.

If you do the above, then you will probably make a mistake; or at least choose a less-than-best idea. However, you will always be progressing. Further, you will also be learning more. As you develop the ideas you select each time you face a challenge, you will learn better how to make decisions: you will get better at imagining the consequences of your decisions and you will be better at not thinking about what might have been. This is better than being in a state of inaction wondering how to choose the best idea, and not gaining experience.

A handy decision-making tool

I have used this tool a number of times when trying to decide to do something or not. Each time it has worked incredibly well. The decision (on whether to do the specific task or not) becomes easy. All you need do is answer the following 4 questions:

1. What's the best thing that can happen if we do this?
2. What's the worst thing that can happen if we do this?
3. What's the best thing that can happen if we do not do this?
4. What's the worst thing that can happen if we do not do this?

Make sure you answer each question fully – especially the 'worst thing' questions. Sometimes we forget that even though things will go wrong, we can fix them. This tool is ideal for when you need to think about trying something or not (a binary decision); however, you can expand it to consider multiple choices if need be. You can also use it outside of engineering too.

5.3.7 A lack of passion

Passion is not something that would likely spring to mind when talking about being a global engineer. But it is probably safe to assume that all engineers have a passion for engineering. However, in this instance I am not talking about that type of passion.

I am talking about the type of passion that might almost be called fanaticism. The sort of thing showcased by Edward Constant II in *The Origin of the Turbojet Revolution* as he traces the ongoing efforts of a small group of people to bring about this new technology.

Much of engineering is the evolution of established technology. It can be significant evolution leading to great gains, but still a development upon what has been done. However, on occasion, such as when aircraft went from piston engines and propellers to turbojets, engineers need to work on that which is truly revolutionary.

When an engineer is working on a revolutionary project, they can expect to be ridiculed by the establishment. They can also expect to face more practical challenges as this new technology is developed.

This ridicule and these challenges can test the mettle of any engineer. If an engineer lacks the kind of passion that allows them to overcome such criticism, then they will likely fail in such circumstances.

And it can be more common for global engineers.

However, it likely will not be a new technology that you need to work on before it is accepted by others. Instead, it is more likely that you will be trying to introduce a superior type of practice from one part of the world to another (which could still be in the same country). In such cases you will likely face similar challenges. People will not like these new ways. People who want to try your introduced practice might still not understand it, and then fail when they implement it. Because they try it the way they think you want them to, but it is not as you intended. Again and again, you will face challenges and setbacks. And you will therefore need a passion for, and a faith in, what you are trying to achieve so that you can push on to success.

5.3.8 Taking criticism personally

This is a good time to talk about criticism. It is a topic that is essential to understand as a global engineer. This is because in some cultures, criticism almost can't be anything but personal.

How criticism is affected by background – and the global engineer

One of the most impressive engineers I ever worked with was a Chinese engineer who had enough insight to realise that when Westerners expressed anger or disappointment it was not at him. The objective attitude towards ideas is very Western – it is a result of the scientific approach that was used in the West since antiquity. In other cultures, like the Confucian culture of China, knowledge is more intimately attached to the individual who put it forward. Thus, people from such a background are more inclined to take criticism personally. In addition, it is odd to people from such backgrounds for someone to become angry with an inanimate object – only Westerners seem to blame their car for running out of fuel and get angry with it; everyone else realises they should have filled up and start thinking about how to get more fuel. The point here is that while we all have a tendency to take criticism personally, some of us can take it more personally. The ability of my colleague to realise that people were not upset with him personally was a credit to him; he showed the characteristic of a true global engineer.

Because we all can take criticism personally and the way criticism can be given varies from place to place around the world, you need to work on your ability to depersonalise it. This way you will be robust enough to work anywhere in the world.

The best way is to turn criticism into a positive.

If you have an idea, and someone criticises it, then it is a chance to make that idea better. A better idea is the product of a better engineer. If you then reflect upon how you came to produce an idea that can be criticised, and then work on being able to produce better ideas, then you will become a better engineer. In short, criticism can be used to make you an even more amazing engineer.

View each new work environment as an opportunity for more criticism and more opportunity for improvement. This can also be a way of taking advantage of people who always criticise to make themselves feel better – they become a source of information to become better!

5.3.9 Inexperience – the new engineer (and those who have not paid attention)

There is something that makes the content of this book easier to put to practical use: experience. It provides greater context, and when you read what is here it is easier to remember a time when you saw something similar happen. Thus, the paradox is that the less you need this book the easier it is to use.

That's not such a big issue though. The real issue is if you're lacking experience and trying to make the most of this book. How can you get the experience to give you the context?

There was a time when everyone who realised that they wanted to become an engineer probably did so after they had interreacted with something technical in the back-shed or some similar space. With this foundational experience you would enter your engineering course with something to which you could attach the theory (you might have also already developed your framing and systemic thinking abilities). However, this is much less common now. And, as I will talk about later, less common in parts of the world where the engineering profession is not associated with the type of activities that provide this foundational experience.

If you are an engineering student (or even thinking about becoming one), then not only do you have no professional experience to put this book into context, but you might also lack any such foundational experience. Doing something to gain this specific type of experience is not only good for making the most of this book, but it will simply make you a better engineer.

Here are some things that you can do now to gain experience prior to working as a professional engineer, and increase your engineering ability:

- Read about engineering – there are many books out there on the nature of engineering and the history of engineering. By reading these, you can learn from others' experiences and get some understanding of what it is like to be an engineer.

- Read engineering-related magazines – popular science and popular mechanics are great ways to find out about new inventions and understand how they work or how they came about. Try reversing the engineering process that was used to develop these new inventions.

- Engineering-themed TV programs – there are not many, but try watching them when you can. If you're a student, then there's a good chance your university will have access to them. Check out the online options too. Programs like *Engineering Connections*, *Prototype This* and *Engineering an Empire* are some good examples.

- Work in the industry as a labourer – this might be carrying heavy items on a construction site or working on an assembly line. It's not engineering, but you get to see it being put into action. Don't just look at what is being made, think about why it is like that and how it could be done better – this is usually much easier when you're working on a production line. Seeing engineering from this perspective is very educational. It would be good if you could do this on a summer holiday or as a part time job, but I do know how rare these jobs are becoming, so appreciate it if you do get one.

- Simply take stuff apart – it's getting harder to fix things these days (companies focus more on cost or production because we usually buy on price), but you can still take things apart to see how they work, how they were made, how they were designed and why they were designed that way.

- Join a group that's doing something engineering like – there are all sorts of groups out there that make all sorts of things just for the fun of it. I know people who build solar cars, catapults, medieval weapons, steam trains, remote control planes, ball handlers – all sorts of things. Joining one will expose you to a few different engineering challenges.

- Make a working model of something – it doesn't need to be a major hobby, but simply going to a hobby shop and buying a complicated hobby project kit will make you look at engineered systems. Think of something like a model plane, car, helicopter or boat (especially the ones used in mini battles). These items are sufficiently complicated, and show you many things about engineering.

- Join online engineering groups – LinkedIn has many of them. Find one in an area that you're interested in. Join and then note the things people are talking about. Look these things up and learn more. You might even get some good connections for your future career if you play your cards right. Another advantage of such groups is that they will put you in touch with other experts. Experts who you might need to call upon. I mentioned earlier that you will at times come across situations where you have no idea what theory is applicable. Knowing experts is ideal in these situations.

- Join a theatre company – I know that this sounds odd, but the only student who ever said to me that he used all of his engineering education worked in a theatre company. The reason for this was twofold. One, he never knew what the theatre company would want him to achieve (a person levitating, a coloured fog, a swarm of bees). Two, no-one else had any technical ability – they just knew what they wanted the effect to be. All these diverse challenges fell on his shoulders alone. If you can find a theatre company with a budget to let you loose and achieve things, then you will have a great time as an engineer and get some serious experience. Not to mention the ego boost – they'll think you're like a real-life wizard.

- Visit technology museums – there are many museums dedicated to specific topics. Some of these have a strong technology focus. One of my favourites is a museum dedicated to firefighting. The history is long. And the problems encountered range from chemical to mechanical to communication to structural to management to electrical. If you go to such a museum, then notice how engineers in the past approached problems given the constraints of the technology at that time. By reverse engineering the process they went through, you gain a more universal understanding of engineering. Try not to focus on what they did, but the thought process that preceded their final designs.

These are just some ideas. However, as you can see, there are things that you can do outside of study and work to ramp up your experience. This will give you some context for the knowledge in this book and any others that you might read, which I would encourage.

5.3.10 Old fart syndrome: too much experience?

This can kick in faster than you might realise. This can be especially so if you are from a culture that has a higher regard for seniority over ability. We all however get stuck in our ways. It's just easier. But, this can compound the conceptual block "That's the way it's always been done". One solution is to always be mindful of the hummingbird effect (mentioned earlier in this chapter). Another is to simply have hobbies – especially ones that evolve without you needing to push their evolution. When you have hobbies, you get your brain into another mode of operation, and this just helps you keep a more agile mind. It can also at times give you a unique perspective on things – an engineering team made of members that each have a different hobby will be inherently more able to produce different perspectives than a more homogeneous engineering team. Make sure you have something outside of work that gets your mind active to break your habitual engineering thinking – which is an oxymoron anyway!

I should point out here that I am not dismissing experience. The more you can have, the better. You just need to ensure that you use your experience properly, to enhance your thinking and decision-making, and not let your experience dictate your decisions.

5.4 Interactions with those around you

Let's now consider how you interact with others. While this book is essentially about how you can be a better engineer, the focus of this section is still worthy of special consideration. Because, this too is a function of your background. As well as the backgrounds of your fellow engineers. What's important to consider is how your interactions compare with good engineering practice. In short: do you act with the authority of an engineer and respect the authority of other engineers?

5.4.1 Authority – doing what you're told when you shouldn't and don't even realise it

Authority can come in many forms. It can also make us do things that we ought not do. The classic experiment, where people were effectively induced to torture others with electric shocks by a researcher in a white coat (and thus having the authority of a doctor or scientist), showed what an authority figure can make us do. This is not likely to be an issue that an engineer confronts at work, but I did say that authority comes in many forms.

What would you do if your boss told you that you should pursue a certain solution, but you could argue that another idea was better? What about using a design solution that is basically the same as the one used by the market leader? Or if someone who has written a book on the respective topic suggested a certain solution? In each of these cases, you have a different type of authority. Any of them could guide the path you choose to take when solving an engineering problem. They might provide good guidance, but they also might not.

The important thing to be aware of is that you are not overly influenced by the authority of others when solving engineering problems. The best solution to this is to rely on facts, which include first principles, and logic. By relying on facts and logic to make all decisions, authority will not have a negative influence on your decision making.

There is a flipside to this. If you are an engineering manager, then note that you might be overly influential upon people working for you. In addition, people working for you might also be over-influenced by established technologies or the designs of market leaders (a little like fixation). You might need to take action to ensure that there is no untoward authority influence.

Anecdote – authority versus first principles

This was the event that made me realise that background could have a profound effect on how we work as engineers. During my research, I interviewed a Canadian electrical engineer who had been working in China. He relayed a situation where his Chinese manager had asked him to pursue a certain design option. The engineer knew, from a consideration of first principles, that this option would not work. The manager insisted and the engineer continued to refuse to spend time on this. The manager then approached a Chinese engineer, who complied – the boss told him to and authority is more about position than expertise in Chinese culture. The outcome confirmed the conviction of the Canadian engineer. However, the manager was more appreciative of the Chinese engineer, because 'he tried', and was not concerned about the time wasted. This anecdote shows how one's cultural background can mean that authority can override good engineering practice. It also shows that your manager, if not an engineer, might not understand how important first principles can be.

5.4.2 A lack of personal authority

The term 'personal authority' was coined by the anthropologist Joseph Campbell. Personal authority is displayed when we take responsibility for ourselves, our actions and our decisions – no matter the outcome. A lack of personal authority can contribute to not being capable of making decisions, but it can also contribute to not fully developing and applying your engineering ability.

If you ever have the chance, then look up Joseph Campbell and his presentations on personal authority.

He makes a very convincing observation that those of us who have higher education (like the vast majority of engineers) have spent so long deferring to others for approval and evaluation of our actions and abilities that we have never truly become adults. We are not prepared to understand the world at a deeper level so that we can take responsibility for ourselves or our actions.

You cannot be an engineer without personal authority. You really have no-one else to defer to; you are the one who needs to be the expert and decide what will be tried.

Ask yourself now if you tend to rely on others to determine strategies to solve problems or if you blame others for your failures. These are signs of a lack of authority. Or are you prepared to take each situation as it comes and you are prepared to trust your experience and abilities as an engineer?

To improve your personal authority, start noticing the outcomes of your decisions and actions and learn from them. Joseph Campbell notes that professional sportspeople often have greater personal authority. They have had the feedback on their efforts from their performance – there is little ambiguity over which team scored the most, who ran the fastest or who lifted the most. This objective feedback is very different from a mark from an educator assessing your subjective abilities; even those that seem objective. A good score on a thermodynamics test does not guarantee that you understand the application of thermodynamics theory such that you can apply it in practice and improve a real system. If you start paying attention to the objective outcomes of your engineering actions – how efficient was that circuit? did that pump last as long as you expected? was it the heating process that caused the cracking? – then you will become more certain of the outcomes of your future actions. You will then have the personal authority that will let you apply your engineering ability.

5.4.3 Negative people – painful but useful

We probably all know at least one person who loves finding problems and pointing out what could go wrong. They have a unique combination of traits: negativity with creativity. They use their creativity in an almost exclusively negative way. These people can be very useful – you know that they will pre-empt all possible issues so you can resolve them before they become real. However, they can also be draining.

The trick is to know when and how to use them so that you get the benefits without the drawbacks.

I have found the best way to 'switch on' these people. I sit with them at a designated time for a designated period and ask them to raise concerns about any proposed idea. I then simply take note of the issues they raise without trying to solve them. Trying to solve these issues while new ones are raised is what's draining. Then, at a later time, I can go through the issues, group them into common themes and decide what actions I will take. This is similar to applying the black hat followed by the green hat in Edward de Bono's Six Thinking Hats method.

The flipside – are you a negative person?

As a general rule, being negative does not go down well with others. Especially if you are viewed as an outsider. You have probably had to work on this in the past to come off as more positive. And you will need to so if you want to be a global engineer. However, there are times when you will want to use this attribute to spot issues to be solved, so never let it go, but do manage it.

5.5 Your perception of the nature of knowledge

You might think knowledge is a fairly simple concept to most people, and that it would be viewed in the same way by anyone anywhere on the globe. However, the nature of knowledge, such as where it comes from and the way it should be treated, can vary a lot from culture to culture. There is even an entire branch of modern philosophy dedicated to the nature of knowledge: Epistemology. Given this, you can imagine that there are many different ways people view the nature of knowledge. Therefore, understanding how you treat knowledge and how that relates to best engineering practice is essential if you wish to be a global engineer.

5.5.1 Compartmentalising

I spoke about compartmentalising when talking about first principles. However, it can actually go well beyond not using the theory you learned while studying in your professional life.

While we often think of engineering as being a technical thing with machines, you can "engineer" other things such as business plans, holiday itineraries and the journey you take when dropping your kids off at school. This means that you can use your engineering skills (framing, systemic thinking and first principles) in other (non-engineering) roles that you might have throughout your life – professional and others.

Many engineers will move into roles that are not exclusively engineering. Management of an engineering team is probably the most obvious thought, but I have seen engineers move into finance, sales and medicine. This gives you some idea of the diversity of roles that engineering can lead to. One of the biggest mistakes that you can make, when moving into a non-engineering role, is to assume that you have few pertinent skills.

Always think about the skills that you have developed as an engineer, and then use them outside of your traditional engineering role.

Doing this has two, almost opposite, benefits. Firstly, it means that you can perform better in almost any role. Secondly, it means that when you're not an engineer (perhaps when you're working in a stopgap job while looking for work after graduation or being let go from a job) you can still take action to improve your engineering skills or to demonstrate your ingenuity. Don't ignore these opportunities.

5.5.2 Overreliance upon your education

There are so many education institutes around the world with so many different approaches that you have to wonder if anyone has yet gotten engineering education right. If they all have a different approach, then they can't all be right: can they? They certainly CAN all be wrong though.

In *The View From Here - Optimize Your Engineering Career From the Start*, Reece Lumsden cites works by economists who found no correlation between the reputation of an engineering degree provider and the career success of graduates. Further, in 1961 a report by MIT actually found that engineering graduates from institutes with less theoretical focus, and lower reputation, provided graduates who often became the managers of graduates of "better" universities. This was because the more practical education allowed these graduates to better evaluate ideas early on (recall sensing tendencies mentioned earlier in this chapter). However, these managers were still reliant upon others for deeper theoretical analysis of ideas (see Eugene S. Ferguson's *Engineering and the Mind's Eye* for more details).

The fact is, you will need to keep on learning after graduation no matter where you studied. There is so much to engineering that no single institute can claim to have taught it all.

Anecdote – what are you meant to be taught?

An academic colleague of mine once told me about a letter (this was before email) he got from an ex-student when working in industry.

The student explained how he had been given the task of designing a gangway. However, he had never been taught the procedure to design such an item. He thus had to use first principles to design it. He then went on to say that he was very disappointed that he had to do this and assumed he should have been taught how to design a gangway at some stage during his education.

My colleague then spent some time formulating a strategic response to explain that no engineering education was that specific. And then to explain that what the student had done was indeed what was expected.

Your education gives you the ability to do almost anything, but you need to decide how you will use this knowledge to be able do it.

5.5.3 Forgetting what you know

This aspect of knowledge (or its loss) aligns well with first principles, but it's not about their explicit application. It's more about realising when these principles are at play and using them to guide you. When you can see them at play in a system, you can use them to guide your thinking about what is possible and the best way to make it possible. Consider the anecdote below as an example.

> **Anecdote – forgetting your own discoveries**
>
> If you get the chance, then read *The Origins of the Turbojet Revolution* by Edward W. Constant II. In this book, the author relays the story of how Osborne Reynolds (basically the inventor of scaled similarity) chose to no longer pursue his steam turbine work due to leakage. A simple consideration of the relative size of the leakage path would reveal that the effects of leakage would become smaller as the turbine became larger. Note that the leakage paths remain relatively constant in absolute size as the overall size of the turbine increases. Basically, according to the scaling laws, as the steam turbine gets bigger it will become more efficient. Reynolds missed the chance to build a competitor to the steam engine because he did not consider the deeper implications of his own discovery.
>
> We can all forget what we know.

The first principles you have learned as an engineer can be applied in many places. In each situation you face, put effort into identifying those principles at play. Then think about what the implications of these first principles are and how you can use them to bring about a better outcome. Recall the 5% thing I mentioned earlier in the book a couple of times? If you do ever hear an engineer say they only use 5% of what they learned, then it probably means that they forgot 95% of what they were taught or only understood 5% well enough to be able to see its application in their employment. If you always think about the implication of first principles, then you will drill them into your memory and get better at applying them in your work as an engineer.

	Engineers	Other designers
Framing	✓	✓
First principles	✓	✗
Systemic thinking	✓	✓
Goal analysis	✓	✓
Fixation	✓	✓
Solution focusing	✓	✓
Coevolve	✓	✓
Creativity	✓	✓
Visualisation with sketching	✓	✓
Opportunism	✓	✓
Modal shifting	✓	✓

Engineers versus designers (a checklist of skills). Notice that engineers share many practices with other designers – each to differing extents, but still shared. However, there is one that is very much the domain of engineers. If you forget your first principles, then you basically forget what makes you an engineer.

5.5.4 Not understanding transferable skills

The nature of how skills from one profession can help in another deserves a book all to itself. However, I can attest from experience, how engineers often need to have more understanding of this transferability than they typically do.

Later, I will talk about how, in practice, engineering is not as universal as one might think. But right now, I am going to focus on how it is also good to know how some skills can carry over in ways never thought of.

To first help you open your mind to this topic, it is worth considering something that was once explained to me by an industrial psychologist. It turns out that a good pastry chef will also likely make a good telephone counsellor. The reason for this is that both jobs demand an ability to respond when needed. A pastry chef needs to act when the pastries have been at a certain temperature for a certain period or when others are ready to be put in the oven. Get this wrong by a small difference in time, and the pastries are not up to scratch. When someone calls a telephone counsellor, that counsellor cannot say "I don't feel like helping suicidal people right now." They need to answer the phone and be ready to help straight away.

If two jobs as different as pastry chef and phone counsellor can have such similar skills, then it would be expected that different engineering roles would too.

However, engineers seem to forget this. I have been guilty of it myself.

Anecdotes: How hard is a job, really?

When I worked in academia, I regularly visited students who were working in industry for practical experience. One of these visits was to an ice-cream factory. Before I visited, I was wondering how hard such a role could be. After I visited, I had a very good idea. Ice-creams need to be made at breakneck speed. However, ice-cream is soft, and cannot be handled too roughly. The chocolate wafers that are often added to ice-creams are frequently delicate as well. The ice-cream will also need to be dipped in melted chocolate and then cooled while using little energy so that the overall cost is low. On top of all that – the machinery used needs to be incredibly clean. As far as I am concerned after that visit, if you can make ice-cream at an industrial scale, then you can do almost anything. However, when students with this experience applied for employment in the rail industry, the engineer reviewing their resume could not see the value in the experience they had. I could not judge – I was once the same.

The same can be said of chocolate. I spoke to an engineer who worked in the chocolate industry and noted that many think of chocolate factories as large lolly shops. If you ever come across someone who works in the chocolate industry, then ask them about tempering chocolate to see the parallels with metal production and the use of design of experiments to see how complex recipes can really be.

Engineers need to be open to understanding what other engineering tasks are like. This includes those tasks in other cultures, economies and environments. It is possible that another engineer will have skills that you would not anticipate at first, and that another might not be as skilful as one would intuitively expect. This understanding is essential for a global engineer who will often be in new environments. Dig deeper when judging other engineers' experience.

5.6 The treatment of information

The following could have been included in the section on the nature of knowledge. Indeed, there is a link between knowledge and information, but the way information is treated will affect the knowledge that you gain and possess. It is this treatment of information that deserves separate attention so you can be sure your background does not have a detrimental effect on your performance as an engineer.

5.6.1 Not understanding standards

Standards can be regulatory, voluntary, produced by professional groups, produced and used within a company (they might be referred to as 'processes'), or picked up informally by the engineering community. They are an essential part of engineering, but not many engineers understand the true nature of standards.

There are four things I have come to realise about standards that are not all commonly known by engineers:

1. They are intended to make some aspects of engineering more efficient.
2. They should be based on sound scientific knowledge that is pertinent.
3. They are made by people who are no smarter than you – I have been on standard committees before, and I know this to be true.
4. They are at least made by people who are experts, but their area of expertise is not always what you might think.

Points 1 and 2 make engineering standards unique. They are used to help engineers design and make decisions; however, they are not a replacement for our understanding of the natural world. Instead, standards augment this understanding. Standards are not a lazy way to design nor are they simply a level of quality to be met (which is what some engineers I know assumed because they had never been properly introduced to standards).

Standards can augment your understanding because of point 3. They codify the expertise of engineers who have worked for an extended period in the relative field. Thus, standards allow you to design to a level higher than your experience or wisdom would normally allow.

This is where point 4 becomes significant. Standards will be developed by people who are expert in the specific area, but these people might also have expertise in other areas. This can influence the final standard.

Anecdote - A relaxed standard?

I know of a standard on electrical appliances that seems to have a relaxed sound measurement procedure. However, a sound expert was on the respective committee. He pointed out that the extra effort often put into to measuring sound was to remove other sources of sound. Without doing this, the measured sound would only be higher. Because the test was to ensure that a maximum was not exceeded, this relaxed procedure would only help to make quieter (and better) appliances. If this engineer had not been on the committee, then the sound measurement procedure would have been much more complicated. Someone who reads this standard might think that the sound measurement procedure would be applicable to other scenarios, but an engineer who ensures they think for themselves would realise that the sound measurement method was not a universal one.

Anecdote - The limits of standards

I also had a related experience where a senior engineer relied excessively on standard boss design for self tapping screws written by the manufacturer of the screws. This senior engineer implicitly assumed this standard was comprehensive, and should be followed universally. However, the standard was only focused on the strength of the fitted screw, and was not focused on mouldability. Thus, following the standard without using engineering expertise would not result in an outcome suited to a moulded product. And this is where the senior engineer came unstuck. The form they designated simply could not be made.

Taking these four points into consideration tells you that standards can be used to make you more productive. However, you do need to understand them to ensure that you apply them correctly to your situation and realise that they can be made better – they were made by people after all.

5.6.2 Not understanding measurement and randomness

Engineers typically understand the importance of measurement. When you have a number for something (after measuring it) you are able to improve it. You can also compare it to alternatives. You can also find the best alternative because, with measurement, you know what the best is.

Without measurement, we know very little.

Once you have a measurement, your understanding of whatever it is you're working on increases phenomenally.

However, it can cause an issue too. Engineers can sometimes become so obsessed with the need for measurement that they seem to think they have either an exact number or nothing.

If you want to learn more about this, then take a look at *How to Measure Anything* by Douglas W. Hubbard. While you can measure anything, and get more insight into whatever you want, sometimes you can only measure with limited accuracy. This is fine as long as you ensure that the conclusion you make, based on these mea-surements, take this uncertainty into consideration. I have seen engineers become 100% certain based on numbers from a handful of less than accurate measurements. Being certain of something that is actually not certain can lead an engineer to make bad deci-sions and waste a lot of time.

Pretty much every number has some tolerance to it. Always think about what that tolerance is and how it should affect your decisions.

Sometimes it is not a number, but a state of being. This can, in turn, affect theories on why engineering systems do what they do. In *Engineer Philosophy*, Louis L. Bucciarelli provides an example of how an engineer can think they know what a system is doing, then predict its performance accurately, but still be wrong in their understanding. He provides an interesting example, but I can cite one from my personal experience in the anecdote below. This is related to confusing opinion with fact (to be discussed soon). Always be sure of what you truly know. There's nothing wrong with theory or estimation, just be sure what they are.

Anecdote – incorrect measure of the state of a system

There was an exhaust system of an engine that was vibrating excessively after a period of operation. It seemed logical that this would be a result the material losing stiffness as it heated up. With a reduced stiffness, the deflection would be greater, and the vibration would have a higher amplitude and lower frequency. The solution was to make the exhaust stiffer by increasing the thickness of key elements. It would then have the stiffness needed at the higher operating temperature. This solution worked, and it was assumed that the problem was properly understood. However, the exhaust also expanded as it was heated, and this reduced the tension on an elastic mounting. As the mounting had less tension, the deflection increased, and the restraining force decreased. A more well-reasoned and better solution would have been to design the mount so that the tension was not excessively affected by the expansion. Sometimes we never know when we have the wrong measure of the state of a system and its mode of operations.

5.6.3 Confusing opinion with fact

This is not unique to engineering. We all do it in one way or another in many parts of our lives. This means that, in general, it's good to ensure that you collect facts when possible and ensure that you know when something is just an opinion.

It is however of more acute importance in engineering.

As I have mentioned before, engineers use knowledge gained through the scientific study of the natural laws to find optimum solutions. This is clearly at odds with simple opinions. Be mindful of this when making decisions as an engineer – especially when you are judging concepts.

> **Anecdote – electronic control of mechanical systems**
>
> When ABS was being developed, it was actually delayed in many areas by mechanical engineers who were untrusting of electronic systems. In their opinion, electronics were not reliable enough. Today, most new cars have ABS and other systems are also controlled by electronics. So these mechanical engineers were wrong. Yet, their opinions were so strong that the development of ABS was slowed. Their convictions came from out-dated experience – when electronics were indeed less reliable. Simply reviewing test data on the reliability of the electronics would have provided the facts, and ill-informed opinion would have played no role. See *Hitting the Brakes: Engineering Design and the Production of Knowledge* by Ann Johnson for more details on this.

W.J. King calls the resolution of opinion and fact the "Let's go see" attitude in *The Unwritten Laws of Engineering*. It's a good attitude to have. If you want to know what's happening with something, then go take a look. It could be returns of products, issues on a construction site, issues raised by end users. No matter what it is, do not rely on second-hand information – have someone with sufficient understanding go take a look. It need not be you, but sometimes it is best that it is. In fact, sometimes it's good for a team of engineers to go look. By having a number of perspectives when looking at something, it is more likely that the facts will be found. In some circles, this would be called a "Gemba Walk" for the Japanese word meaning 'real place'.

Having a desire for facts over opinion can also help with your ability to apply first principles. Opinions are more aligned with statements like:

- That should work.
- I think that's a good enough length.
- Surely that will stay cool enough.
- I can't see that working.
- It worked before so it should be okay.
- The boss asked us to do this.

Learn to hate statements like these. When you do, you will be more inclined to use logic to reach a more specific conclusion. This will in turn require you to ensure you have solid grounds. You will then be more motivated to apply first principles, which is the first step to mastering this aspect of engineering to become a global engineer.

An exemplar of the "let's go see" attitude - Joseph Bazalgette

Joseph Bazalgette was a civil engineer charged with modernising the London sewerage system in the 1860s. To do this, he had to first track the flow rate of the Thames, which was affected by the tide, and the speed with which water would flow at an incline. Then he could design a system capable of taking the sewerage far away enough for the Thames that London would be safe. However, before he did this, he needed to know why the existing system was not working. After about a decade of the London Metropolitan Commission of Sewers failing to come to any action on the problem, Joseph Bazalgette went into the sewers himself to ascertain the problem. That's going to see! The episode of the *Seven Wonder of the Industrial World, The Sewer King*, gives an excellent dramatisation of the project.

5.7 Chapter summary

As I mentioned at the start of this chapter, it has had a negative focus: those things you should avoid. It has also been long – there are a lot of things to avoid. Nevertheless, it could prove to be one of the more useful chapters. While it is reasonably easy to recall what you should do, the bad habits covered in this chapter can return unnoticed. Returning to this chapter in the future would be a wise move – especially if you find your development has halted or even regressed.

6.

Becoming a Global Engineer

Engineering is one of those degrees that can take you around the world. That's one of the many reasons why it's a desirable qualification to have. However, you still need to understand engineering as a global profession if you do want to take full advantage of this opportunity.

The key to being a global engineer is adapting to different situations. When you're in a new situation, think more intently about how the situation is different from others in your experience. Ask why people might be seeing problems differently from how you see them. Based on this: what information do you need and how do you need to start thinking about things? Do you need to step back and collect more information? Do you now need to consider different constraints? Do you need to frame problems differently? By doing this, you can utilise your fundamental skills, which have been covered earlier, in any location – making you a global engineer.

This chapter will drill down into the types of differences you might encounter so that you will be well prepared for any situation you might might encounter around the globe.

6.1 Is engineering universal?

In some ways, engineering is universal. Not only are the laws of physics common around the world, but so too is much of the technology we use. This second commonality (technology) is influenced by the laws of physics, so you would expect technology to be common. This commonality is also brought about by the fact that engineers are required to find an optimum solution. Less optimum technologies are soon made redundant and replaced by the optimum. The superior technology then becomes common around the world too.

In fact, if there was another world in the universe somewhere inhabited by intelligent life, then you could reasonably expect that it has been through or will eventually go through a period where its technology is much like ours. Now that's universality.

However, there is more to being an engineer than knowing the laws of physics and understanding the optimum technology of the time.

If you were to work in another country, then you might find that the way you present your ideas or think about problems does not align with your colleagues. They might think you always miss important or obvious issues, don't spend enough time developing your idea before presenting it, or perhaps developed it in the "wrong" manner. This is about how people approach engineering problems. It is an aspect of engineering that is not universal and can make it difficult to be a global engineer. While much of engineering is global, this aspect of problem formulation is not.

6.2 Background – what made you the engineer that you are?

Background can affect your ability to perform as an engineer in sometimes obvious and sometimes very subtle ways. Sometimes your background can actually help you. Sometimes your background helps you in certain circumstances, but then works against you in others.

By understanding how your background can affect your engineering ability, you can do one of two things. The first is to avoid situations where your background is a liability, and stick to those areas where it is an asset. The second is to realise your areas of weakness and take action to strengthen them while still nurturing your strengths.

I obviously hope that you take the second path. However, the first path is still much better than paying no attention to how your background affects your engineering ability. By understanding how background can affect engineering ability, you can be as capable as possible of taking whichever path you choose.

6.2.1 Cultural background

What is your cultural background? It is possible that you have a bit of a mixed background. It is possibly a mix of more than two. But even then, one of them is probably dominant. This can affect the way you think, the way you approach engineering and your engineering ability.

I am not talking about thinking with regards to basic values such as respect for parents, attitude toward authority, the importance of money, or the kinds of ceremonies and pastimes you engage in. However, I should point out that they could be linked. I am talking more specifically about two things:

1. How your cultural background affects your attitude towards knowledge.
2. How your culture can dictate what you think engineering practice and development should be.

6.2.1.1 The nature of knowledge

Your attitude towards knowledge will affect the way you apply first principles and your ability to frame. By understanding how your attitude towards knowledge does this, you are much more able to take action to improve these abilities.

At this time, I want to point out a few aspects of culture that you need to keep in mind when I talk about how these can affect your engineering ability. Keep in mind the following:

- When we compare cultures, we are not comparing the extremes. If, as you read this, you find that you are from a culture that encourages a certain characteristic when compared to another culture, then do not assume that this means your cultural background makes you as strong in this characteristic as possible. There are no limits, that I am aware of, on how extreme a culture can be. There is always room for improvement so don't let your culture make you complacent.

- Remember that culture is a part of your background. It is not in your genetics. It can have a very strong influence and feel like it is latent, but it is simply an environmental effect that you can change if you truly wish to.

- Do not think that I am telling you that you must turn your back on your culture. The point here is to understand when and how it might affect the way you work as an engineer. By doing this, you can then choose how you wish to use your culture. I will talk more about how this change can be confronting, but also how you can manage it.

- Do not assume that you are typical of your culture. You have probably met someone who was fascinated with a culture other than their own, and was desperate to immerse themselves within it – an example of how people can have other cultural influences. It is possible that, in some key aspects related to engineering, you are not typical of your culture. Be aware of this possibility so that you can use the content of this chapter to the greatest benefit.

- Similar to the above, do not assume others are typical of their culture. The content of this chapter can be of great assistance when working in multicultural teams, but remember to treat each member as an individual. Also, realise that others, like you, should be on a journey of improvement, and they can be expected to change with time and practice.

So, which culture do you associate with most? There are many, but I will keep it fairly general. Do you think you fit in with any of the following?

- Confucian
- Western
- Arabic
- Hindu
- African (Maybe specifically North, South, East, West or Central)

It is possible that you might think it's a mix. I have a colleague who is Bangladeshi and describes himself as a Muslim (Thus he has an Arabic influence) from Hindu culture. Many in South East Asia would potentially describe themselves as part Arabic and part Confucian. Others might think that other religions need to be added to the list to describe how they see themselves. Finally, some will feel that they have done their best to rid themselves of all such cultural influences and subscribe more to economic or political descriptions of their culture and values. This is all possible; the list is intended to make you think about what you believe your background is. More importantly, you need to think about how your background affects your attitude towards knowledge.

To date, the reported research into how culture affects engineering ability via the attitude towards knowledge has been limited to comparisons between Confucian and Western engineers. This is because there have been a large number of Western engineers working in China. The large number of engineers who had worked in mixed teams in China (and could comment upon what it was like working with others from different backgrounds) made this comparison the ideal one for the investigation. Hopefully, there will be more comparisons in the future to inform us more about how we can develop our engineering ability. For now though, let's focus on the comparison of Western and Confucian cultures with regards to knowledge and engineering practice.

As the name suggests, Confucian culture reflects many of the teachings of Confucius. On the other hand, another name for Western culture could be 'Aristotelian'. For a long time, Aristotle was the oldest known thinker to have influenced Western thought via the ancient Greeks. Although people before Aristotle are now known we still use his name to describe this type of thinking. It should be pointed out that Confucius claimed that he was only summarising what had been said before him. So essentially, they are just names, but by considering the teachings of each, we can better understand the philosophical foundation of each culture.

In short, Confucius spoke about how one should behave toward others and to show respect for elders and the past. Also in short, Aristotle spoke of how to use a logical process (involving argument) to find an answer to any question one might have. Confucius spoke of harmony and Aristotle wanted to dig deeper and change the way the world was seen. Because Confucius spoke of respect for elders and the past, he implicitly suggested that knowledge comes from within us – older people of the past would know more. Aristotle implicitly suggested that anyone could come up with the right answer and that the argument was what mattered.

When Western and Chinese engineers work together, we see comments that reflect this. Chinese describe Westerners as crazy because they get so emotional when things do not work out as planned (as they logically should) while Chinese try to maintain harmony. Westerners note how Chinese feel uneasy expressing their ideas when they are junior or, when they are senior, not accepting that an idea of theirs can't work. The position and authority of an individual implicitly affect the quality of ideas for Chinese whereas westerners would argue with theory and supposedly objective knowledge regardless of position.

The previous two paragraphs make up just an example to help you become aware of how you can use your understanding of your background to determine how it might be hampering your engineering thinking. To make the most of this example, think now about your cultural background. Is it one that puts the emphasis upon the importance of the argument and logic behind an idea or does it put more importance upon where the idea came from?

If you are in the latter group, then you might find it hard to take a problem given to you by another and then reframe it, especially if the problem was first framed by your boss. You might also be more inclined to try remembering a solution to a problem – as opposed to looking for the underlying theory and then applying that as required to the problem.

If you think you're from a culture that relies more on logic, then you can't still assume that you are always logical. We have ALL made the mistake of thinking something correct because we thought the person telling us had enough authority, and we really should have thought more before blindly trusting them.

Basically, remember this: A good engineer will use objective knowledge and logic to evaluate an idea. This is regardless of where an idea comes from. This means that until it is tested, any and every idea should be considered and evaluated. It might be a very fast evaluation, but the idea is still given the respect it deserves, and it gets an evaluation.

6.2.1.2 Engineering practice

What is an engineer? We covered this earlier and I gave what I think to be a good definition. However, I know that it is open to interpretation:

- Is engineering a trade or a profession?
- Do engineers use their hands or their minds?
- Where do engineers work - factories, offices, mines, oil rigs, on the land?
- Physically, is engineering a clean job or a dirty job?

The answer to each of these questions is the same: all of the above. Engineering can take many different forms depending upon the company and industry that you work in. Because of this diversity, it is easy to find someone who will support any of the options provided.

A note on trades

Some engineers have also formally studied to be qualified tradespeople. This is not what I suggest all engineers do; however, pre-trade courses would probably be a good idea for most engineers. I want to ensure that no-one thinks I am suggesting that engineering automatically includes a respective trade. Trades are distinct and deserve respect for what they are. Much of the wealth we enjoy today, while once relying much on the input of engineers for development, is now only maintained by the efforts of tradespeople. We would likely notice the absence of tradespeople much sooner than the absence of engineers. One should not assume I am being dismissive of the effort one needs to apply to become a tradesperson when I later suggest that engineers will need to engage in comparable activity to become a good engineer.

This allows the definition of engineering and its practice to vary from one part of the world to another. What can have the greatest effect is the attitude toward professionalism. In some parts of the world, professionals would risk their reputation if they dared to touch hand tools or get their hands dirty, or even use their hands - upper class professional types just don't do that. In other parts of the world, there is much less distinction between the regard people hold for different types of employment. An engineer in such a place would damage their reputation if they were not prepared and able to get their hands dirty - 'An engineer is someone who washes their hands before they go to the toilet' (an anonymous quote I have heard numerous times before). Some places can almost be anti-intellectual and not appreciate that there is even value in contemplating theory or thinking prior to simply trying something to see if or how it works.

These different cultural views towards the actions of a professional, what a professional is and what they would do daily affects how different cultures then in turn see engineering.

I would go further than to say that the answer to the above questions is 'All of the above.' I would say that the answer should be 'Engineering *should* be all of the above.'

As I have already discussed, the evidence has shown that a good engineer is one who can sense situations and phenomena broadly. They are visual, tactile and auditory – 'sensual' as Eugene Ferguson says in *Engineering and the Mind's Eye*. This means that a good engineering education system will expose an engineer to a number of practical tasks. It also means that for an engineer to continue to develop, they will need to have a sufficient diversity of experiences so that they can say they have experienced each of the options in the above questions.

If you come from a culture that discourages professionals from using their hands, then you will have a weakness to overcome. If you come from a culture that has anti-intellectual tendencies, then you too will have a weakness to overcome. You might think that you will choose to specialise in one approach, and be so good at it that you will be able to overcome any deficiencies in ignoring the other approach. The issue is that there is little research to show that is possible. You simply learn more and faster from approaching engineering from both the theoretical/intellectual/professional side and the practical/sensual/trade-like side. You will need to strive for balance so that you have a greater understanding of engineering practice – no matter your cultural background.

6.2.2 Economic background

Research into the influence of economics on the way people view problems shows the following: If you are from a developing country, then you are more interested in low-cost products that are reliable and do what they are meant to do; however, if you are from a developed country, where you can afford everything that you need, then you are more interested in products that are different from others.

The research mentioned above comparing Chinese and Western engineers found that this carried over to engineering as well. Western engineers noticed that Chinese engineers were very good at redesigning products so that they were much easier to make while still being able to perform the desired job. However, the same Western engineers also thought that the Chinese engineers, because they were so focused on the need to keep production smooth and reliable, were not interested in trying out new product variations. This was despite the fact that more sales would be had with an innovative product because it was being sold to Westerners. There was also evidence of Westerners being so caught up in the desire to create something new that they forgot their design actually had to work. Note that the natures of the economies have changed since this research so what you extract from this should be only about economic influences - not nationality influences.

There is an interesting observation to be made here. Engineers tend to work the same way regardless of what is required. This is much like the goal analysis I spoke about earlier. Engineers from developing economies will be more likely to set a goal of low cost and ease of manufacture and engineers from developed economies will be more likely to set a goal to be new and innovative. If the goal chosen fits what is needed, then this is perfect. However, in any other case it will reduce the quality of your work.

Think about your economic background (this can also be affected by your industry or company, and not just your country). Has this made you always approach each problem the same way regardless of what was really needed? Are you too focused on cost or too focused on novelty? In either case, try in the future to understand what is actually needed and work accordingly.

6.2.3 Environmental background

Environmental background could include economic background, but because economic background was so significant I treated it separately. Nevertheless, because your economic situation can affect your environment, there will be an overlay between economic background and environmental background. Environmental background is more a product of where you have worked and the type of environment that you were raised in.

For example, some engineers have worked for years in a company where all engineering tasks were broken down by a manager into smaller tasks for engineers to then work on. Engineers in such environments tend to be very detailed thinkers, and have trouble thinking systemically when they move to a role where that is required. They do develop this skill, but it takes time.

Another example is engineers who grew up in rural communities or even on a farm. Such engineers have had much experience with machinery and getting things to work by any means necessary. In India, this is called a 'Jugaad' or 'work around'. With a background like this an engineer can become very tactile and find a solution that will work at that time, but: will it be suitable for a product that needs to be mass-produced; will it allow for servicing if required; do others know how to use it?

Of course, growing up in any environment can have an effect. I recall an engineering colleague who grew up working in his father's factory where much of the machinery was operated by linkage mechanisms. As a result, he always thought about using pulleys and levers. He would always avoid hydraulics or electrical control. Sometimes this was just what was needed, at other times he created machines that were not remarkable for what they did, but for their complexity given the relatively simple task.

The point I am making here is that our environment, be it from growing up or where we have worked, can affect the way we choose to approach a problem. To be a better engineer you must not only understand the problem, but also understand what kind of solution process the problem requires. As you get better at this, you will do it automatically. However, it is always worth keeping the following in the back of your mind: you might be choosing a certain approach to solve a problem because of habit (from your background) and not because it's what the problem really needs. Think about what the problem really is and what it really needs. And never be afraid to realise that you're mistaken, and need to use a different approach.

6.2.4 Organizational background

Organisational differences can often come from similar sources as those mentioned. For example, a company might have a culture that is a result of the economy of the industry. The auto industry has very different economic conditions from those of the caravan industry. Differences might also be a result of the culture of the host country. I have noticed that engineers who work for German companies, regardless of the country that they are working in, have troubles with concurrent engineering, but do have excellent technical ability. This stems from the German culture of relatively strict organisational structures that are to be adhered to and encourage exceptional specialisation. This contrasts with the experience of people working in Japanese companies where open communication for concurrent engineering and lean production is often encouraged instead.

An organization can also have a significant effect on your ability to develop your expertise. Some companies will have a culture where theory was something that you used to pass your degree, but not for work. These engineers will tell you that theory will rarely work – recall the earlier section where I spoke about how some people would convince themselves that theory doesn't work in the real world instead of admitting that they don't know how to apply theory. In such companies, this becomes a self-fulfilling prophecy, and no-one there will ever be able to become an expert engineer unless they actively go against the prevailing culture.

Be mindful of how the companies that you have worked for are affected by the industry and the environment of the head office and how this might affect the way you have been thinking as an engineer. You might need to counter this when you move into another company or simply to become a better engineer.

In *Designing Engineers*, Louis L. Bucciarelli gives an excellent example of how this can happen. An engineer who was accustomed to working with devices that respond at high speed (electrical systems) made less than optimal assumptions about the appropriate time steps for a simulator that was used to simulate an engineering system that operated much more slowly (a thermal system). The simulator was recalculating for every fraction of a second while simulating changes that took close to a day. The simulator was considerably slow until a more suitable time step was used. This is not an extreme issue, but it is interesting to see how one's background can change the way we see things. Louis calls this our 'Object World': the way we use natural laws and engineering experience to understand that which we work with.

Eugene S. Ferguson makes a similar observation about a tyre company designing a space station that was essentially a giant car tyre tube. In *Engineering and the Mind's Eye* Ferguson argues that the engineers of the company in question could not help but see almost everything in terms of pneumatic tubes.

Richard West, author of *Performance at the Limit*, has attributed Toyota's failure in Formula 1 to the effects of organizational background. Toyota is excellent at producing well-documented and well-tested vehicles at low cost and in large numbers. However, they did not do so well when they needed to produce only a few cars and quickly modify them to sort out unforeseen issues as they presented throughout a racing season. Because of related fundamentals, you probably could not expect the Ferrari F1 team to be able to mass produce a large number of low-cost high-quality cars. Congruent with this, I have personally seen ex-F1 engineers struggle with understanding the comprehensive systems needed to produce a large number of vehicles at a low-cost and high quality.

These are examples of how young and experienced engineers can be hampered by any background. I am telling you this so that you can counter it. It is not an excuse for bad habits or providing a reason to assume another engineer can only do what they have always done. I have a colleague who happens to have to deal with this issue a lot. He works in a medium-sized company where engineers need to take on a large number of tasks, but he employs many engineers from large companies that have each engineer specialise in an area. It takes effort at times, but he can change them: and they work well. If they can change, then so can you (and other engineers).

6 .3 Further examples of how engineering is not universal

To further show how your background can make it difficult to apply your engineering skills in other parts of the world, I want to share some examples I have personally witnessed. If you know an engineer who has travelled and they seem to be the kind of person who notices such differences and their causes, then ask them what experiences they have had.

6.3.1 Water in Australia

I recall a German associate once being very critical of how poorly Australians used grasslands and other flora to provide insulation around homes. They considered the layout of many Australian houses to be very poor. However, unlike most of Europe (and much of the world) Australia is so dry that water security (ensuring there is always water available) is sometimes viewed as a greater risk than global warming. The benefits of reduced energy use and carbon production do not justify the lost water.

6.3.2 Large projects in China

Given its size, China rarely does anything on a small scale. This includes its engineering. I have had Chinese question the numbers I have put on a request for quotation for something I designed – 'Yes, I really do only need that many in a year.' I have also seen relationships between Chinese factories and Western design firms break down after the factory supported a design firm by producing prototypes only to then find out what kind of quantities were actually expected at the start of production.

What can seem like a large-scale engineering undertaking in one part of the world might not seem that way in another. This can change the decisions an engineer will make about the allocation of resources to a project or the assumed resources that can be called upon later. Not understanding the relative size of your engineering task and the associated resources can cause many issues for you when in a new environment.

6.3.3 Professionalism in India

In India, engineering is deemed a profession and as such those who are engineers are often not expected to ever touch hand tools or equipment, much less know how to use them. I mentioned this earlier, but I will repeat it here given the times I have noticed this effect. Certainly it is not always the case, but I have worked with engineers in a Western context where the saying 'An engineer is someone who washes their hands before they go to the toilet' often makes sense, and found that the same saying could shock Indian colleagues.

An expectation that you will make and physically implement your own ideas yourself can be a shock to an engineer who has come from a place where there were always others to do that work for them.

Recall how culture can affect physical engagement in developing an engineering intuition and complete understanding. The type of thinking style that is suited to having others take on the physical work will be different from that where you must do this yourself. Are you less tactile than you could be because of where you have worked as an engineer? Do you need to put more effort into thinking about theory as opposed to always trying something out after spending years in a 'build and try' environment?

6.3.4 Adaptive engineering in Africa

Some period before writing this, I had a long series of conversations with an African engineer about engineering design. I was very hopeful of doing some research with him on the issue we were talking about, but we never got the funding. Nevertheless, the conversation was an interesting one - it provided the following insights.

In much of Africa, many aspects of life are not stable. There could be a major change that would make many assets into liabilities. You can't take a factory with you if you need to relocate due to natural disasters or war. The result is that all solutions need to be implemented quickly and get that immediate job done. This leads to some remarkable ingenuity. However, engineers who excel in this environment find it hard to start documenting their ideas so that they can be implemented numerous times or think about their ideas within the context of the mass production of industrialisation. Therefore, it becomes more likely for any job, no matter its nature, to be thought of as a new job. There is reduced codification of engineering tasks, which in turn reduces the opportunity to build on and improve earlier engineering systems. In such an environment as an engineer you will be starting almost from scratch each time or working with what you have available and little more.

6.3.5 Is engineering a trade? Australia versus Europe

Australia has a reputation for being egalitarian. For this reason, engineers in Australia do not have much natural or assumed authority over tradespeople. In Europe, engineers are very highly regarded. I had a conversation with a European engineer who told me of his shock when coming to Australia that tradespeople would contently change an engineer's design while implementing it. In Australia, if a tradesperson notices an issue during implementation, then a change can be made on the go. This can make the implementation easier, but there might be unforeseen issues beyond the comprehension of a tradesperson, and the new design might not be well documented for future reference and further development. Further, this could encourage engineers to be less systemic in their thinking when designing; any related issues can be sorted out on the day. This is an example of how culture can indirectly affect engineering cognition.

6.3.6 America Versus Europe – the air wars and race car wars

There are two great books that I have read about the engineering aspects of the development of turbojet aircraft. One of these is *The Origins of Turbojet Revolution* by Edward Constant II. A part of the book is dedicated to a comparison of the developments in the US and Europe of aircraft during the 40s and 50s of the 20th century. The major difference was that US aircrafts were larger and fitted with more comforts while being capable of longer flights. The European aircrafts on the other hand typically exhibited greater speed and efficiency. The difference in flight was attributed to the more capitalistic nature of American society and the geography. As a result of the economic and geographical environments, the engineers ended up viewing the needs and opportunities of aircraft development differently.

This likely is still evident today. I relayed this story to a colleague of mine who works in the aerospace industry at an event to encourage mathematics in high school students. He felt that to this day the same difference (although maybe not as evident) between Boeing and Airbus was present.

And another example. A fellow engineer who was raised and educated in Belgium, worked in F1, and now works in Indie cars in the US, made a similar observation about the drivers for engineering effort. In the US these drivers were more a result of commercial needs. In Europe, where companies seemed more secure due to a different economic environment, there was usually a desire for general performance and purest technological improvements.

Spending time in either environment would change the way an engineer would frame a problem and the systemic issues they would consider. For example, an engineer moving from one place to the other would need to consider if there is a shift in the balance of focus between:

- efficiency and performance to produce an optimised product
- speed of development to ensure competitors do not take market share.

Taking that bit longer to optimise a design might not be wise if sales, and thus cash flow, is diminished; leaving less funds for development. However, producing a design that is less than optimal for a mature market, where most existing offerings are optimized, will likely lead to failure. You do need to understand what is really important for your current environment and situation as opposed to simply doing what you have always done in superficially similar situations.

6.3.7 New Zealand manufacturing in China

This example also shows of the value of concurrent engineering. When I was working in China, I was given the task of helping a client (from New Zealand) find a suitable supplier for a product they had designed by a design company in New Zealand. The original design called for blow fill sealing (where a plastics container is blow moulded, filled with content and then sealed in a continuous operation). This operation was easy enough to source in New Zealand, but in China at the time it was relegated to pharmaceutical manufacturers who would not manufacture this product (it was not a pharmaceutical product). The New

Zealand design team had assumed the manufacturers in China were the same as those in their home country. Thinking more globally and not assuming the world is not the same all over would have helped, but so would good concurrent engineering practice.

6.3.8 Indian particularity and Englishmen aggressiveness

This is an anecdote shared with me by a colleague who worked in the confectionary industry as part of a large international company. His role was to produce trial products developed by the R&D departments in the English lab and the Indian lab. As part of this he had to work directly with the two development teams as the respective products were made in the trial production line he was operating. This offered a chance to see two teams from different cultures take on essentially the same task.

What were the observations?

The Indian team took a very methodical approach to setting up the production line. This is indicative of the caste system, which still has influence in India as its commonality diminishes. One of the defining features of the caste system is that parents would teach their children how to apply the family trade. This was very much a watch and repeat process for many aspects of many professions and trades, which is a very efficient way of training in such a context. The English team on the other hand was viewed as aggressive: when they confronted a problem, they formulated a theory and quickly tried it to resolve the problem.

My colleague was of a similar background to the Englishmen, although he was not English, and was more comfortable with their approach while he sometimes had to suppress his desire to suggest the Indian team doing things differently (more like what he would do). His ability to acknowledge that it was a different approach from what he would do, but would still get the job done, is indicative of successful global engineers I encountered while doing research into this area. What probably helped him do this was a naturally polite disposition that compelled him to first understand others and what they were doing before commenting. It's a good trait for a global engineer to have.

6.3.9 What are your examples?

The previous subsections are just some examples. These differences will not necessarily always remain. Economies and cultures can change. The point is that if you wish to be a global engineer, then you need to focus on the fundamentals and be aware of how and why things are different in other parts of the world.

It is often hard to do, but try spending some time thinking about the habits that you might have as an engineer that are actually a result of where you have worked. We often assume that these habits are simply aspects of good engineering. The habits seem so obvious to utilise that we can't see them as anything but good practice. This is why it is hard to correctly identify these habits.

If you can't think of any habits, then at least be open to the chance of them being present when you do work in another part of the world. I have worked with many engineers who were, at the time, working in other parts of the world and who did not have this ability. They instead made bigoted assumptions about the locals, which you can imagine did not make them popular, and they never really learned all that they could from the experience of working as an engineer where many of their assumed rules no longer held. It was truly their loss. Trust me; you do not want to be like this.

Trying to understand why other engineers think the way they do, and then from that understanding why you think the way you do, is a brilliant way to understand yourself as an engineer. And that's an excellent help to becoming a better engineer.

6.4 Working backwards to be a global engineer

We often take for granted, and don't seem to fully consider information that has been given to us, until we have a real need for it. This is one of the reasons why project-based learning is becoming common in engineering degrees. Once you have struggled with a problem, you pay intense attention to the person or book or other source that has the knowledge that you need for that problem.

Therefore, you will probably not really think to develop the skills you need or even think to ask how to develop them until you find yourself in a situation needing those skills. This is at odds with modern educational practices you are familiar with: where the goal is to teach you all that you may need to know prior to knowing what you need. However, the sense in not worrying about something until you need it is logical. This, I have found, is key to being a global engineer: quickly understanding what skills you need or the way you should be thinking when in a new situation.

Thinking about the implications of being in a different situation is easier said than done. You might (probably will) make mistakes, but at least you're working at being a global engineer.

One last point on this: don't assume that I am saying that you must work like those around you. It might well be that you can teach them something useful too – many of us forget this. Being a global engineer should be a two-way street of influence and betterment. Try also looking for commonality in engineering as well. In *The Existential Pleasures of Engineering* Samuel C. Florman argues quite effectively that it is a natural human trait to engineer, and that we can all gain that same sense of pleasure as we do. Combine the sharing of knowledge with this shared pleasure, and you will be even better placed to be a global engineer.

7.

The Book in a Nutshell

Much about being an engineer is managing your thinking – thinking about how you think.

We live at a time when there have been many excellent engineers before us. Also, there have been others who studied these excellent engineers to understand what it is that makes them excellent. This means engineers like us can learn how to emulate their characteristics to become better engineers ourselves. And that's the essence of this book – monitor your own thinking based on how you now know the best engineers think.

The best engineers were:

- able to see the problem in a way that allows them to see the engineering solution,
- able to use their scientific knowledge to optimise their solutions, and
- always considering all aspects of the system to look for opportunities and to understand the true challenge they face.

By working on these abilities yourself, you too can become an excellent engineer. One who will be an excellent engineer no matter where they are: A global engineer.

But you must also remember that things do not always go smoothly or according to plan. Sometimes, you learn as you go. As good as it is to understand a problem first, you sometimes need to start trying to solve it before you really understand it. And you will probably never do this alone so you need to be in a team: a team where everyone knows what everyone else knows and what everyone else is thinking.

You will need all of these skills to be an excellent engineer. However, depending on where you are in your career, you will need some skills more than others. Always think about what you need more (or less) of.

This can be very much a function of where you have been and where you are now.

Understanding this is what will make you a global engineer. Sometimes you have learned skills that have served you so well in the past that you can't help but think they are obviously what all engineers should have. Sometimes they aren't even skills, but simply habits or attitudes. By being able to observe these objectively, and adjusting them to suit the situation at hand, you become a global engineer.

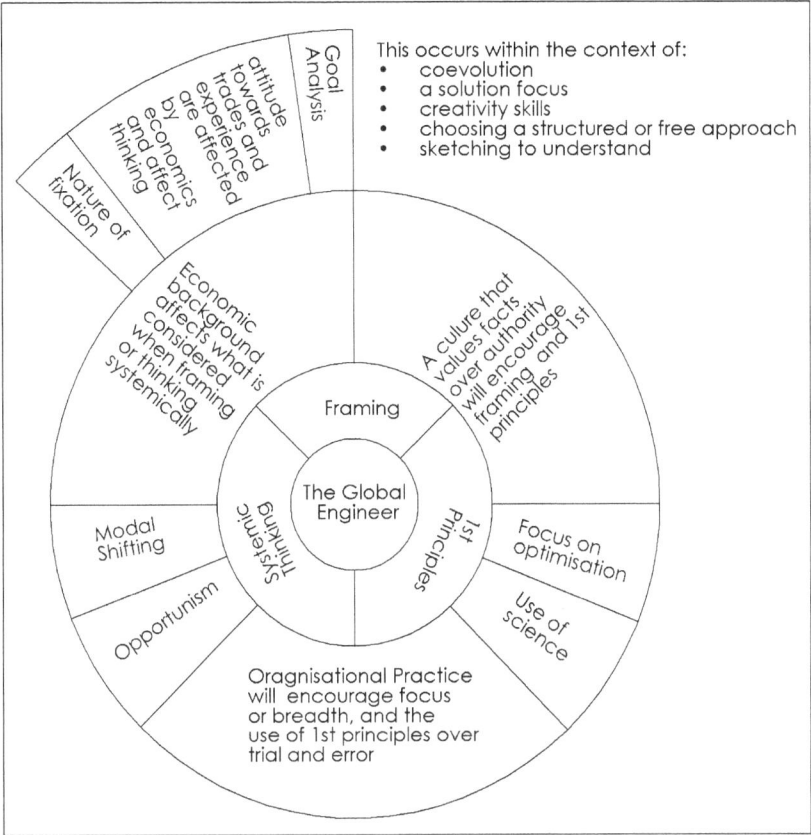

The diagram above is a graphical summary of the book. If you ever feel that you need to quickly review the book for a specific reason, then look at this. You can use it to jog your memory. You might then know what you need to do or what to read to refresh.

To keep progressing your development as a global engineer, take part in the conversation at www.cjsteele.com

8.

References

This is not a complete list of references that I have used when writing this book, but they are the most influential ones. I have covered them in enough detail so that you know what I got from them and you can decide if you want to read them as well. You will note that I have provided the ISBN along with the author and title – the ISBN will always be the easiest way to get the edition I used, but by all means, access whichever is available to you.

1.1 Books - engineering

These are books that are readily available and would be ideal for any engineer's library.

Hitting the Brakes: Engineering Design and the Production of Knowledge by Ann Johnson (ISBN: 978-0822345411). This book is fascinating. It is written by an historian and uses the development of antilock braking to understand how engineering communities develop. It provides great insight into how knowledge in engineering is developed and shared. As you read this book, you will notice how and why your understanding of different technologies you work on changes over time. Ideal for engineers involved in a rapidly changing industry/technology.

The Existential Pleasures of Engineering by Samuel C. Florman (ISBN: 0312141041). This is a good book to read for a unique perspective on engineering. At the time of its publication, engineering was not held in high regard. This book was a response to that. Thus, the book feels a little dated. Nevertheless, it does help develop a better understanding of what engineering is and how it fits into society. Well worth a read.

What Engineers Know and How They Know It: Analytical Studies from Aeronautical History by Walter G. Vincenti (ISBN: 0801845882). This book was a bit slow to get started for me. However, it was fascinating to see how engineers tackled different problems throughout history. It uses the aeronautical industry as a case study, but much of the content is applicable to all engineering. At the end of this book, you will start to think about what kind of an engineer you are and if perhaps there are some things you could do a little differently.

The View From Here (Optimize Your Engineering Career From The Start) by Reece Lumsden (ISBN: 1450750559). This is a book unlike any other I have come across before. It is the only book on engineering that starts at choosing a place to study engineering and then considers how to manage your engineering career. It does not talk much about the unique characteristics of engineering, the way other books do. Still, no matter the stage of your career, this book can likely help. This is a book that will make you reflect upon your past as an engineer and think more about what you should do next in your career.

Designerly Ways of Knowing by Nigel Cross (ISBN: 3764384840). I, and a number of other writers, have argued that designing makes up the essence of engineering. In this book Nigel Cross has covered what is known about design cognition (at the time of writing). It is not uniquely about engineering; however, if you want to get a good understanding of what design cognition is, then this is probably the best book around. After reading this book, you will start to monitor yourself while you work as an engineer and notice all the different design cognitions you perform as an engineer.

The Unwritten Laws of Engineering by W. J. King (ISBN: 0791801624). This is an old-fashioned book, but one that is good to read through every now and then. Each time I do, I am reminded of something that I should do more of.

Designing Engineers by Louis L. Bucciarelli (ISBN: 0262522128). The best thing about this book is that it introduces the concept called 'the object world' (it was at least new to me – you might have come across the concept before). This is the world of engineers and how they choose to view it as they solve their problems. I found this book hard to read, which leads me to assume the author simply has a very different writing style form my own. Therefore, if you found my writing hard to read, then you might like this one. It sheds much light on the nature of engineering and how to be good at it. This book will always make you think about the level of engineering development your industry is in and what needs to be done next to progress understanding within your industry.

Engineering Philosophy by Louis L. Bucciarelli (ISBN: 9040723184). This is a little like the sequel to Designing Engineers. It also talks about the object world, but it goes into much more detail about the nature of engineering. It talks about the social nature of engineering; how we, as engineers, can sometimes think we know something and do not; and how engineers learn. At the end of it, you will probably think twice before ever reaching any engineering conclusions.

Engineering and the Mind's Eye by Eugene Ferguson (ISBN: 026256078X). This is one of the most visually rich books on engineering. Because the book essentially argues that visualisation is the key to engineering, this makes sense. The book argues convincingly that engineering requires mostly visualisation, but still a tactile understanding. It cites many other sources to support its contention and was the first book I read that finally explained the link between art and engineering. If you want to gain a better understanding of how engineering has developed, from the beginning to what it is today, then this is an excellent book. After reading it you will probably start thinking about how you can improve your engineering ability through the senses you use when confronting a problem and how you choose to represent that problem.

The Origins of the Turbojet Revolution by Edward W. Constant II (ISBN: 080182222X). This book focuses, as the title suggests, upon the development of the turbojet. It deals substantially with how ideas of a revolutionary nature often come from people outside of the respective industry. How revolutions can push some companies and their engineers to the side line and raise others. These revolutions are rare, and a book about one, written by an historian, is a useful insight into the engineering tasks and attributes essential for such revolutions. What I found most interesting about the book was that it also covers the development of the antecedent technologies like the water turbine and supercharger.

How we Got to Now by Steven Johnson (ISBN: 1594633932). This book tracks the development of 6 major inventions that significantly changed our world from the perspective of how they came to be through interactions with other technologies and societal events. If you need to work on your ability to understand how and why the time can be right for a new idea, then read this book.

The Saturn V F-1 Engine: Powering Apollo into History by Anthony Young (ISBN: 0387096299). This traces the history of the titular engine and the mission to the moon. Along with coverage of the technology and it's development, there is also much in here about engineering behaviour and management for success.

1.2 Books – non-engineering

These are books that are relatively easy to acquire and might be of interest to any engineer wanting to improve their abilities.

Influence: the Psychology of Persuasion by Robert Cialdini (ISBN 006124189X). This book has become a classic in marketing circles. This is what makes it a tragedy. The author was trying to help people not be persuaded unduly by salesmen, advertisers and conmen. He did this by explaining how the techniques work. Thus, salesmen, conmen and advertisers buy this book to learn how to influence others. This book though is ideal for engineers who want to be aware of how other factors can make them deviate from what is the best solution.

Six Thinking Hats by Edward de Bono (ISBN: 0316178314). This is certainly no longer a new book. However, it is an excellent book that helps you consciously look at problems from multiple perspectives, and be more certain that you understand it.

Willpower: Rediscovering the Greatest Human Strength by Roy F. Baumeister and John Tierney (ISBN: 0143122231). Engineering is easily one of the hardest professions to enter. Becoming a better engineer is not easy either. In both case, one needs willpower. This tells you pretty much everything you need to know about how to improve your willpower for whatever it is you wish to improve.

Talent is Overrated: What Really Separates World-Class Performers from Everybody Else by Geoffrey Colvin (ISBN: 1591842948). If you thought engineers were born and not trained, then this book will make you think otherwise. If you need more convincing that you can improve your engineering, then this is the book you want. It's ideal for anything else you want to improve.

Choke: What the Secrets of the Brain Reveal About Getting It Right When You Have To by Sian Beilock (ISBN: 1416596186). Engineers usually have time to make their decisions and urgency is rarely an issue. However, this book also talks much about how the way we see ourselves affects the way we perform. If you, or engineers who work for you, are potentially limiting engineering potential through assumptions of capability, then this will show it need not and what can be done about it.

How to Measure Anything by Douglas W. Hubbard (ISBN: 9781118539279). This is almost an engineering book, but it's also a business book. The reason why I put it in the list is because of how unique it is. There are few books out there that help you deal with uncertainty the way this book does. Given how many things can seem uncertain at the start of an engineering project, this ability is ideal for all engineers to own.

Thinking, Fast and Slow by Daniel Kahneman (ISBN: 0374533555). This book provides great insights into how our initial thoughts can often be wrong. Essential for good engineering – especially when you are working with something new. It also provides insights into when you can rely upon your intuition.

1.3 Papers

There are also many other papers out there, and this is just a sample. However, they make the foundation of much of the theory covered here and are worth noting.

Akin, O. (2001) 'Variants in Design Cognition' in C., E., Newstetter, W. and McCracken, M., eds., *Design Knowing and Learning: Cognition in Design Education, Elsevier Science*, 105-124. The best thing about this paper was how it compared engineering with other types of designer. This really brought out those things that make engineers unique.

Bhawuk, D. P. S. (2009) 'Intercultural Communication in a Dynamic Environment: Preparing Managers of Developing and Developed Countries Using Cultural Standards', *Progress in Development Studies*, 21(2), 161-181. This paper is focused more on business, but it provides a great link between cultural background and the expected actions of someone from such a background.

Cross, N. and Clayburn Cross, A. (1998) 'Expertise in Engineering Design', *Research in Engineering Design - Theory, Applications, and Concurrent Engineering*, 10(3), 141-149. This can in many respects be considered the paper that started the whole idea of developing engineering expertise. This was the paper that focused on engineers of unquestionable talent.

Ehrlenspiel, K. and Dylla, N. (1993) 'Experimental Investigation of Designer's Thinking Methods and Design Procedures', *Journal of Engineering Design*, 4(3). This paper looked into only experienced and novice engineers; however, the methods used were rigorous. Many of its findings pre-empted those of Cross and Clayburn Cross.

Hubka, V. and & Eder, W. E. (2003) 'Pedagogics of design education', *International journal of engineering education*, 19(6). This paper was brought to my attention when I was researching. One of the authors was a reviewer of a paper of mine and upset I had not cited them. I had not done so because they were within a different group of researchers. Thus, it was interesting how this paper presented similar findings to those in the papers I was aware of. Providing some confirmation on what has been reported in this book.

Newing, A., van der Waal, S. and Steele, C. (2012) 'The effects of background upon engineering design expertise – a Sino occidental comparison', in *International Conference on Advanced Design and Manufacturing Engineering, Taiyuan, Shanxi, China* . I am a little biased because I was an author of this, but I do think it shows how our backgrounds can affect our engineering design ability much more than we would realise.

Salas, E., Cooke, N. J. and Rosen, M. A. (2008) 'On teams, teamwork, and team performance: Discoveries and developments', *Human factors*, 50(3), 540-547. This paper summarised pretty much all that was known about how to get the most out of a team at the time of its writing. If you want a quick good introduction into what makes a team work, then this paper is perfect. It's an excellent example of a good literature review as well.

van der Waal, S. Newing, A. and Steele, C. (2015) 'The nuances and management of multinational design teams: A Sino and occidental comparison', *Journal of Integrated Design and Process Science*, I am biased about this one too; once again, I am an author. However, this includes a lot about the issues that can be encountered when trying to get a multinational team (of engineers and designers) to work together.

Acknowledgements

The initial drafts of this book were reviewed by a number of fellow engineers who took considerable time to read it and offer feedback. I would like to acknowledge them now.

- Mary Sangas
- Haryadi Herdian
- Robert Ellison
- Daniel Sheehy
- Michael Goodwin
- Santiago Corujeira Gallo
- Paul Wellington
- Bryon Spells

I would also like to acknowledge all the others I have worked with over the years – giving me the insights that allowed me to write the content of this book.